Who Will Survive?

The teenager's struggle to win the *ultimate* battle!

Steve Fitzhugh

Dedicated in loving memory of Eva Mae Fitzhugh, my mother. What a great woman! You loved me enough to often remind me that I am somebody. In your own way, you convinced me of my purpose and destiny.

And

To Dr. Ronald J. Fowler. What a great man of God! Thank you for introducing me to Jesus Christ. Through you I've learned that it's not so much "who" I am as it is "Whose" I am. In Christ I have discovered divine purpose, and destiny.

This work could not have been completed without the tireless patience of my wife, Karen. Thanks for your input, multiple readings, and support. Thank you Nicole and Siona, my beautiful daughters, for giving me the time I needed to write. Thank you to our dear friend Hollie Hardison for typing this manuscript. A special thanks to my editor and godmother Carol Ann North. Your double duty as editor and intercessor pushed the work to completion and covered it in prayer.

TO:

Teenagers and the wonderful people who raise them:

May the story to follow heighten your awareness of the war in the heavenlies over the souls of young people. My prayer is that this book brings enlightenment that can easily be applied to decision-making, and may your decisions in life honor the great Creator, the Lord God Almighty.

INTRODUCTION

The plight of the 21st century teenager, ruled by peer acceptance and lost in the haze of conformity, grows darker each day. Where are the solutions? Who has the answers? When will our nation's young halt self-destruction? When will teenage homicide cease and desist? When will the constant brigade of sexually transmitted diseases among teens vanish? When will the number of babies having babies disappear?

Clearly we live in one of the most challenging periods for teenagers to come of age. Young, impressionable minds are being exposed to extreme measures of vulgarity, rebellion, lust and perversion each day. Materialism, sensuality, and greed punctuate the dreams, goals and desires of the young. The television media and music industries instruct our students in the "ways of the world". These mediums – in sync – effectively reflect almost an elaborate, well-coordinated scheme designed to sabotage the tomorrows of our most precious ones, the children, our future.

Who Will Survive is written with several premises in mind. Suppose the bible stories are true. If so, there really is an all-powerful, all knowing God who, in spite of our circumstances, remains in full control. With this premise in mind, we recognize that there exists a devil and his name is Satan, who thought that the crucifixion of Jesus Christ was his greatest victory. However, it was the crucifixion and subsequent resurrection of Jesus Christ that proved to be Satan's insurmountable defeat.

In the following story, the intriguing, insightful, and disturbing events provoke parents and students. Although categorized as "fiction", the realities of life dominate the content. Many of the scenarios of the personalities within find their genesis in the lives of the teenagers with whom I've known in my extensive travels. The United States Justice Department, Children's Defense Fund, and the Centers for Disease Control provided many of the facts, figures and statistics. Each entity deals with real life, revealing factual data. Essentially, <u>Who Will Survive</u> brings true untold life stories to a reading public. Rather than entertain the reader, I intend to enlighten and challenge them. For some readers, this book serves as a warning. Success in the 'ultimate battle', the battle for eternal life, determined by **choice**, creates tensions that drive me to write this and other books. You must choose everyday to survive. To survive is to overcome. To overcome is to win the ultimate battle and secure a victorious life. The question remains, "Who will survive?"

FOREWORD

One night a couple of years ago, I prepared to go to bed. As I sometimes do, I turned to the 11 o'clock evening news to catch the day's headlines. I was saddened to hear again of the consistent, tragic end of another teenage life. In another story, the depressing, hopeless cycle of teenage hardship was investigated and reported. By the news' end I was so moved I could hardly sleep. In fact, I was so overwhelmed with a particular thought; I began to write it down. The inspiration was heavy and fast. I wrote as quickly as my hand would move in an attempt to keep up with the story unraveling in my head. When I looked up at the clock, it was 8 o'clock in the morning. I had been writing all night. Half of this book, <u>Who Will Survive</u>, was written.

There are two ways I'd suggest you read this fascinating little story. It is an easy read and not too long. It has plenty of drama and makes you see things differently. I suggest the first time through you read it in one sitting. Because it is short, the average reader should be able to finish within the same time frame you would watch a television movie. If you cannot read it in one sitting, try to complete it with as few interruptions as possible. That way the flow of the mindset it takes to understand the story will not require as much mental adjustment. Keep in mind, since it is written from the perspective of the evil side of life, what is said to be good, in our understanding will be something bad. Any mentioning of the "Enemy", in real life, is not our enemy but our friend. The second time through, try to write down, and then look up all of the research references referred to in *"The Book"* of this story. Read the entire reference before continuing with the story. When you read a promise, memorize it and try to discover other promises not mentioned in the story. Memorize them as well. Finally, what survival strategies would you offer the teenage characters in this story? Are you an "Agent"? What relationship do you have with the Teenage Task Force? Think on these things as you read. And if you know of a student or parent that needs to read this book, pass your copy on to them. Sometimes saying the right thing in a different way makes all the difference in the world. I hope you enjoy your reading of, <u>Who Will Survive</u>?

Steve Fitzhugh

CHAPTER 1

Quietly, the host of the dark side gathered around the Evil One's lair to discuss the recent setbacks. Somehow, the Holy One succeeded again in fulfilling His plan of reconciliation. Another teenager, Satan's highest target, now rests anchored in the word and testimony of the Lamb of God. Another teenager defeated Satan, by crossing over to the Kingdom of Light, and working now to fulfill the great commission as an Agent of the Most High. Oh, how this disgusted the Evil One. Though he tried not to show it, his disgust was only the cover for his true emotion. Blood curdling fear usually gripped his heart whenever a target, particularly a teenager, escaped to the path of righteousness and life.

Somehow the zeal of the young has been harnessed by the Holy One and transformed by His Spirit into the fire of revival. In every time, every generation and every millennium, the young seem most eager to defy the gates of hell. A few centuries ago, three young, Hebrew friends, who because of their defiance and escape from a fiery furnace, changed the course of biblical history. David, merely seventeen, was selected to establish a mighty kingdom. Gideon, the youngest of his brothers and sisters fought mighty battles. And Mary, a virgin, surely no more than fifteen, became the mother of the One called King of Kings and Lord of Lords. All were everyday people. All were ordinary people. All were teenagers, youth of their time, their day.

Deep in the recesses of the spirit world, the dragon himself calls his cohorts to an urgent strategy session. His smoldering lair was dark and sulfuric. Thousands of demons hissed about, but only the royalty would sit at the table of doom. The entire room quickly grew quiet and still. An eerie, almost numbing, uneasiness swept through each demon as the chief dragon himself, Satan, that cursed serpent, entered the room. Markedly hideous, unequivocally evil and particularly disturbed, the devil began to speak, slowly, coolly and deliberately. "Murder courses through my veins right now," he said, "and the power to destroy at my talon-tips. Anticipation of openly dismantling one of you, to demonstrate my complete and utter disappointment over the course of what happened last night, pumps my heart with wicked fever! WHOMEVER stands responsible for that ghastly combination of events, give me an explanation, NOW!" he exclaimed.

"It was I, sir" spoke a demon, the leader of the forty-fourth regiment, trembling with a timid, quivering voice. "I underestimated the power of prayer."

"HOW COULD THAT BE?" Satan shouted in disbelief. "YOU BUMBLING IDIOT! How could you overlook or underestimate the power of prayer? How, after that blasted Elijah at Mount Carmel? HOW, after Moses at that Great Sea? How, after the madman in Gadara when his legion were cast into the swine? How, after she, who only had to touch the hem of the garment of the Nazarene, was made whole? HOW... COULD.... YOU.... UNDERESTIMATE... THE... POWER... OF.... PRAYER?" Satan stood and menacingly stretched forth his narrow gruesome hands. Rage contorted his face and neck as he changed into a hideous hue of red and black. "SIEZE HIM!" Immediately hundreds of annoying demons seized the leader, shredding and ripping him to pieces. Within moments slimy remains of the nasty demon were scattered throughout the room.

The previous night planned years in advance, by the "brain trust" of the dark side began as expected. A young, innocent eleventh grader disconnected with his friends, buried with low self esteem, and ignored by everyone in his life, except his five-year-old sister, prepared to leave the home for the last time. His sister, though much younger and less mature, noticed something different in her brother's eyes as he left the house that night. She could not discern or recognize the spirit of suicide upon his face. For Satan had coached Suicide throughout the entire evening, resorting to some of his most faithful schemes. That night, Satan expected to confront a lonely teenager who appeared stripped of his personal sig- nificance. Such emotional lows provide a rich soil for the seeds of seduction from Sir Suicide and Duke Depression. Satan did not, however, expect to contend with the simple, yet powerful, words quietly whispered by the victim's innocent little sister just after her brother left the house.

"Dear God," she spoke softly that night, "please pro- tect my big brother as he goes out. I love him so much and I love you God. Amen."

While sitting in his car teary-eyed on a lonely deserted road just outside of town, with the barrel of a 357 magnum aimed at his head, hosts of angels immediately flooded his mind with countless reasons to live. Good thoughts, happy thoughts, fun thoughts, strong and lively, one by one attended his consciousness. Sir Suicide, blinded by the light of the angels, and Duke Depression, paralyzed by fear stared into the night. They then frantically departed not wanting to be consumed by the fire in the wings of the mighty warring hosts of God. The angels, under direct orders, proceeded to rescue the boy. The Lord of hosts put into motion his plan for the life of the young man, a plan to prosper him, a plan to rescue him, a plan to build a future with much hope. The Holy Spirit took complete control right then, right there in his automobile on that deserted road. Repentance came quickly that night. The boy abandoned his hopeless suicidal solution and returned home…changed forevermore. The sweet and simple prayer of a little girl God answered in a grand way. A young boy, in an instant, changed from endangered species to Agent of the living God. The enraged Prince of Darkness stormed his chambers.

"TEENAGERS! Hear me!" Satan spewed. "Thirteen-years-old, fourteen-years-old, fifteen, sixteen, seventeen-year-olds… I want older and younger. It doesn't matter what the age. GIVE ME TEENAGERS!" He screamed. "I want their minds! I want their desires and dreams. I....I want their good looks, gifts and talents. I want to spoil them individually in order that I might disqualify them from ever being available mates for each other. I want their futures and possibilities

and the generations yet inside of them. I WANT THE YOUTH!"
He bellowed. "I want to dictate their standards, yes, and fill
their heads with lies and pervert what little gospel they've
ever heard. I want to discourage them from ever being near
those, those, those *true* saints and those *true* sanctuaries of
holiness. I WANT TO DESTROY THEIR WILL TO WIN!" Satan
paused. "I just don't want them to know it is I...doing all of
the destroying."

CHAPTER 2

Satan calmly addressed his hordes. "You all know, of course, how the destruction of the Kingdom of Light depends entirely upon this work. I must assume, therefore, that the findings and intentions you report all reveal your thoughtful preparation. Lord Deception, as the demon in charge sir, you may begin. Present your strategy at this time." Deception prepared to detail his assault plan. As a peculiar demon, he seized every available moment to destroy, trick and deceive. He never appeared as the monstrous demon that committed such destruction. When sinister he exuded innocence. When murderous, he behaved lovable. When vicious, he began harmless. When ruthless, he appeared compassionate. As a master deceiver, he knew full well that the *best* deception contains obvious elements of the truth, and he knew the truth. Since the beginning of time he served close to Lucifer, who was then the angel of light on God's holy mountain. Deception was a truth bearing angel, who echoed the truth to Lucifer as he orchestrated praise to the Holy One. More loyal to Lucifer than the Lord of Hosts, Deception himself fell prey to Satan's trickery and joined him in eternal banishment from heaven and the presence of God. Since then Deception faithfully serves his evil master through the cleverness of deceit.

"I gathered pertinent information at a moment's notice of the honor of your appointment, your Excellency." Deception boasted. "I began my preparation by comparing my most recent findings with consistencies throughout history. All that I am to report…"

"Enough of the preliminary remarks," interrupted Satan. "My time," Satan caught himself, "*the* time is short," he added.

"As you wish Sir", Deception continued. "Although times have changed, the place we must wage war, the battlefield for the lives of the young ones, remains the same. My research tells me that the one called Paul, whom you know, identified the battlefield in the Holy Scriptures."

Satan stood to his feet, pounded his fist on the table of doom and exclaimed in a loud voice, "HOW MANY TIMES MUST I WARN YOU? Make no references to that book of lies!"

"But Sir," cried Deception, "This book remains as the principal source the enemy uses to train and educate our victims."

Satan paused, "I am well aware," he said. "It's just that I hate the sound of that word 'Holy'. Henceforth, if you must make references to that text, refer to it as…. uhh….*The Book*. Yes, that sounds much better. Just…*The Book*….Go on!"

Deception continued. "As I stated before, Paul revealed to us the battlefield, as I am sure you well know, in the letter to the Philippians, section four, paragraphs eight and nine. He says 'think on these things'. Now I won't bore you with the detailed list of what 'these things' were as referred to by Paul. Suffice it to say that the *mind* is the battlefield and serves as our primary target."

"Do you have any other information to support your claim?" Satan asked.

"Yes, there's plenty. They believe that which defiles a man depends directly upon the character within, according to Matthew's writings, section seven, and paragraph twenty. Then again in the letter to the Romans section twelve, paragraph two, they also believe that ones entire life experiences regeneration when ones mind tastes renewal. The mind is critical, sir."

"So what do you suggest, let us see how well I have taught you?" Satan asked impatiently.

"All of our efforts should center on the following three simple goals. If we succeed in these three simple goals, we cannot lose. First, design paths of wickedness to gain access into the minds of the youth. There are several gates that could be used as our entranceway. The ear gate relates specifically to all of the different modes of music, song and spoken word our young targets enjoy. The eye gate serves as the access route for all of the images captured by the eyes. This includes movies, television, internet and everything else grasped by sight. The last gate deals with the unseen vision, the imagination. It is there that we conjure up false images that support our work. The gates represent our various access routes or highways you could say. Once inside, the mind will be our playground as well as foothold to reach our ultimate destination, the heart. Number two, we must establish and reinforce our doctrine by repetition and the casting of improper images against the eye of the mind. The combination of these successes will fortify our principles of destruction. Eventually these strongholds will incapacitate the mind, and when they do, voilà...we will enjoy unbridled access to our victim's center, and life, the heart. For out of ones heart the issues of life flow. With our forces controlling the heart, our doctrine in place and strategic images internally visible, we'll assign your demons and legions to stimulate and manipulate the youth. Our teenager's polluted, corrupted and wounded heart will bleed disappointment all over their very own lives. Isn't that exciting?

They will, unknowingly, forfeit their destiny, execute *our* schemes and, of course, contaminate the pursuit of holiness by others. With our presence infiltrating the mind, ruling the heart, and darkening the vision, even when personal destruction is obvious, rebellion will simply override all logical resistance to evil, or as they say anti-social behavior. By that time, rebellion, our standard will simply be a way of life."

"Hmm," Satan pondered for a moment then asked, "Tell me Deception, what risks jeopardize this scheme?"

"Well," said Deception, "just the, er...uhh...*usual.*"

"What do you mean the usual?" Satan responded.

"Just the problems we've, huh, you know, we ran into in the past." Deception reluctantly stated to his master.

Satan leaned forward. "Deception if you don't identify exactly what risks put our work at jeopardy I'll rip your tongue right out of your deceiving little throat and you'll be silenced forever!"

"Very well sir...its The Truth, sir." Deception whispered

quietly with baited breath.

"What do you mean, the Truth? We've handled the Truth before. We can cover it, hide it, and disguise it. Why I've even nailed the Truth to the cross," Satan chuckled.

"Dear sir," remarked Deception with seriousness and pause, "might I remind you that to believe the truth suggests one thing. Many even here believe it and tremble. But to receive it poses quite another situation. If one believes and genuinely receives the truth, their belief seals our doom."

SMACK! Satan, remembering his days as Lucifer on the Holy Mountain of the Lord of Host, backhanded Deception across the room. Lucifer's vivid memory of the power of the Truth sorely reminded him of his terminal condition - DEFEAT!

"WHO IS LORD?!" Satan demanded.

"SATAN IS LORD!" shouted the room full of demons and imps and fallen angels.

"WHO IS LORD?!" he asked.

"SATAN IS LORD!" they repeated. Deception slowly stood to his feet after lying ashamedly on the floor. Satan turned to him rapidly and roared."CAREFUL DECEPTION OF THE WORDS YOU SPEAK! I-SHALL-NOT-EVER-BE-DOOMED!" he lied. "Do not EVER speak those words again. *I* am all-powerful and *I* will reign eternal as Lord of all! Now Deception, TELL ME YOUR PLAN?"

"At this point allow me to present to you the Teenage Task Force," Lord Deception responded still a little shaken. "First, the Spirit of Corruption." Sire Corruption stood up to report. This grotesque captain of rottenness could not bear the foulness of his own stench. He sat alone because the horrendous stink of his personal space polluted the atmosphere. He spoke articulately, describing an elaborate scheme.

"I, along with my flock, intend to infect every image of godliness, ever exposed to each victim. Whether on television, the radio or in person each preacher will appear as a lunatic, fanatic or hypocrite to our young victims. The impression of the church after my manipulation will dishearten our young victims from involvement. I'll saturate the lives of the adult believers with mediocrity, so as to make the path of righteousness and church itself, abhorrently unattractive to our young targets. When the pastors maintain a greater commitment to political correctness than righteousness, when the parents flaunt infidelity, and the church finds itself preoccupied with happiness rather than holiness, our victims yield as easy prey. My reports all suggest that inexperienced youth fail to recognize even my simplest ploys. After I, Sire Corruption, execute my perfect work, a neutralized defense system of the mind makes the average teenager perilously vulnerable to my assaults. *Shields down* one might say. No more black and white, only gray. I promote a negotiable morality and a rationalize immorality. I blur the line between right and wrong and encourage only what feels good, what looks good and what seems good. Any questions your evilness?"

"But what of our young targets" asked Satan, "How specifically does corruption impact them? Can I identify your touch there?"

"Certainly, subtle at first, you know a little cheating here and a little cheating there. A small theft today begets a little lie tomorrow. Then again, a little sneaking here, and a tiny compromise there. All quite subtle as I said initially, happening almost undetected. But corruption simply and quickly becomes widely accepted, even the norm. My strength lies in my stealth. As long as I remain uncovered my strength grows. Therefore I seek to avoid confession, acknowledgement, or any other source of light that exposes my true nature. Denial provides me with all of the permission I need to transform a tiny fault into a catastrophic failure, even in the good kids. Thus seemingly insignificant cheating will certainly lead to dishonesty, lieing, bribery, and stealing. Eventually all of my wicked underlings roam freely throughout the battlefield and then quite naturally, the heart. Defilement, first on the inside then when it's too late…exposed! Like a painted tomb you could say, white on the outside but rottenness and decay within!

"Bravo," said Satan. "Why can't all of you be as diabolically charming as Corruption? Who's next?"

"Our next presentation comes from our strong man. We call him our 'strongman' because once he establishes his stronghold, any demon that follows takes pleasure in total occupation and victimization of the battlefield. The more secure his foothold, the more profound our activity. The broader his success becomes, the more expansive our enterprise. The swifter his advance moves, the greater our advantage. With the strongman in place, the direction of the victims thoughts, actions, behaviors, standards, dress, language and consequently future, or lack there of, lie totally in our hands," explained Deception.

"Where is this strongman? Who is this strongman?" asked Satan anxiously, rubbing his crusty hands together with excitement and anticipation. "Bring him forward, enough delaying!"

"There's much envy of the strongman. Needless to say, we've had to disguise him, even for this meeting that others might not conspire to attack him. He is vital, yet subtle; his health is our greatest concern. Our success is paramount to his participation. I'll whisper his name to you, and then others from the Teenage Task Force will usher him in, your wickedness." Deception requested permission to approach Satan's throne of brimstone. With permission granted he knelt near Satan's ear and whispered, "The strongman, sir, is Rebellion."

Deception knew that the offer of eternal life from the Holy One was just that, an offer, a gift. Central to the rejection of that offer and consequent dominance by the dark side was the student's own free will to refuse the offer....deny the gift. A rebellious mindset or a position of opposition to one in authority would prove vital. A student can never experience their god-given destiny if at the very core of their disposition they defy, resist, or buck established authority whether earthly or heavenly. Thus the strongman...Rebellion! Every act of rebellion denies God's gift. Almost every teenage miscue takes its instruction first from Rebellion. The premature teenage parent rebelled against God's standard of sexual purity. The argumentative teenage son or daughter, rebels against God's standard of respecting ones parents. The incarcerated teenage delinquent rebelled against God's standard for the respect of laws and authorities. There's nothing new under the sun. The historically strong correlation between rebellion and undesirable consequences, demands that the strongman at the table of dooms' Teenage Task Force be...*Rebellion.*

CHAPTER 3

Deception motioned to the task force. They ushered in a very, very large demon wearing all black. He wore a black hooded cape, black boots, and a black cover for his face that only revealed his pitch black eyes. His long narrow hands, drooped as he walked. His talons, long and far-reaching compared only to the chief demon himself, Satan. The demons throughout the room hissed in vehement jealously. Slowly, Sire Corruption and other members of the Teenage Task Force ushered Rebellion before Satan's wicked throne. He spoke in a deep and mighty thunderous voice.

"Greetings, your Excellency. I humble myself to stand in your wonderfully, horrible presence. Perhaps my plans for the young ones will please you."

"Speak, dear sir. I know your work and I have been pleased in the past. How will you work for us now?" asked Satan.

"I have been afforded a great luxury, unholy one. The teenager, so easily distanced by the church, longs yea, yearns for esteem, belonging, satisfaction and pleasure. I too employ the use of the powerful and impressionable imagination. Youthful lusts inflamed in the mind through fantasy, stimulates a wealth of perversions. Though they do not know it, I take residence in the music, the television and the movies, not to mention other mediums. I ignite the flame of fantasy. I promote a world of make-believe. As we speak, the consuming passion of the commitment to *self* burns strong in the hearts of the young. I destroy goodwill by establishing an entire enterprise of self-gratification. I harvest what feels good, what tastes good, and what looks good in the minds of the youth. After much practice and help from Lord Deception, I can enter the battlefield, the mind, without ever being noticed. For you see, I am disguised among and ride upon the words and phrases of the wide variety of rhythms and syncopations of the popular melodies. To the student I am no more than an attractive beat or a creative melody. They often fall for my disguise, dismissing me merely as just another #1 chart topper. By their own approval, they welcome me into the intimacy of first their ear, and eventually their heart. Tell a lie? That was my idea. You need love? That came from me too. Cheat on your girlfriend? That's my cue. Run away from home? Gotcha! That was me too! You name it. Virtually every notion of anti-social behavior came from my song, my video, my movie, or television show. I partner with my friends Anarchy and Chaos. Almost every week our collaborations appear as the new #1 spots on the music, movie and video charts. Even technology has been on my side. There once was a time when I couldn't even make it into a home for there was only one record player or radio per household. That one radio, parked in the family room, and monitored by parents denied me uncensored access. Times were tough for me back then. Ah! But today, dear Master, huh, huh, huh, huh, it is soooo unbelievably easy. Thanks to modern technology, I can speak through a portable radio, cassette player, or what they call compact disc, over and over and over again. Through miniature computers and digital formats even a device as small as your fist, sir, I can speak literally thousands of messages. I speak blatant heresies against the heart and will of the Enemy and I sabotage the future happiness of our victims, without interruption. You may find this difficult to believe. But these useless excuses for air even *memorize* my precepts without even trying to, just by *singing or rapping along.* Throughout the day they recite *my* norms, *my* principles and *my* standards word for word! Without an understanding they actually rehearse my vices. Rehearsal brings perfection, any fool knows that. I am so good, by the time most finish high school, they can't live without me. When they get into the car they turn to hear *me* on their favorite radio station. Before they go to bed they adjust the radio dial to fall asleep listening to *me.* Even in the malls, they spend what little money they have to take *me* home with them on their favorite compact disc. With the use of headphones, no other voice can compete with *me* for their attention nor interfere with *my* conditioning of the young targets. The classrooms, the school bus, the family car, a crowded mall, the vacation road trip, at the bus stop, even Sunday school, sir, all immediately become private counseling sessions between the victim and me, with the simple assistance of a *headset.*"

"Forgive me master-demon," Satan interrupted. "You can't convince me that you are sowing these kinds of seeds of destruction right under the watchful eyes of the parents. I've heard your lyrics and your insinuations. You promote violence, suicide, illicit sex, abuse, abominable perversions and the like." Satan mentioned with a smile. "Why even some of your interludes between songs are easily x-rated. They're horridly devilish, I should know. It's absurd to think you have the kind of access today that you suggest with these minors, under the watchful care of loving parents and guardians! Keep it real with me Sir, keep it real!"

"My success confounds even me, Nasty One! I'm enjoying great freedoms thanks to these *busy* days. Some products have "explicit lyrics" warning labels but that's just a political joke. It's the students purchasing the products and parents simply just don't check. Rarely ever do parents monitor my activity. They have no clue as to what messages their allowance money buys through the hands of their child. In fact, I'd venture to say, it's oft times *too* easy, I'm completely unchallenged. In those rare instances where the parent raises a standard the child then treats the parent as the enemy. This causes so much friction in the relationship the parent generally gives in and we win again."

"Excuse me hidden demon, may I add something here?" asked Deception.

"Go right ahead", Rebellion obliged.

"The operating belief system that the Strongman instills at this young tender age of life establishes a necessary and useful foothold. The beauty, Lord Devil, is that with each passing year of life this foothold is more hardened and defined. As the adolescent reaches adulthood, the intensity of rebellion now becomes a stronghold. The percentage rate of our targets that escape to the path of righteousness in adulthood sharply and dramatically falls. Even our Enemy understands this and according to the writings in Ecclesiastes section 12 paragraph one of *The Book*, He exhorts, 'Remember *now* thy creator in the days of thy *youth...*' Most new Agents, recent statistics identify a figure near 80%, become so before the age of twenty-one. More specifically, somewhere between the ages of 7 and 13 the path of righteousness sees its largest influx of new Agents. From the age of 13 and following, the numbers begin to fall off. That's why, Sir, this particular demon is our DOC for this population, Demon Of Choice. You may continue Evil One," Deception insisted.

"With absolute free reign on the battlefield, I, the Strongman, conquer the young students mind. I condition it to adopt my horrible ideals unaware. The victims eventually succumb to chaos, resistance to all authority, me-first and me-only thinking, unruly thought and dress, resistance to order and structure, and finally, complete anarchy of the mind. They rebel! And they rebel hard! They rebel against every authority figure and question every rule. No teacher goes unthreatened, no police officer unchallenged, no school principal unaware of my investment in the young. The very entity our Enemy establishes in the home to guide, train and instruct our young targets, the parents, initially receives the brunt of teenage rebellion. All of this wonderful nonsense, simply as a result of the seeds I've sown. Parents don't detect my domination until it's too late. They don't catch on until my talons pierce so deeply into their children's hearts that they become hard as stone. Any parents' advances at this stage normally falls on ears I have deafened and hearts I've hardened. I find it quite amusing, as is often the case, when a parent petitions the church for prayer concerning a rebellious son or daughter only to return home that very day and enable my work through non-involvement.

And if I fail with conditioning through music, which I rarely do, I can always rely on the visual, the video."

"Explain your use of video to me, sir, please?" Satan queried with mischievous anticipation. "Now this is getting good," he snarled with naughty laughter.

"Video helps me to compliment my words and phrases by painting images on these young, foolish, innocent minds. Words alone do not impact with the devastation as words with an image. From the beginning of time with hieroglyphics to modern day overhead projectors, chalkboards or PowerPoint, the visual arts amplify education. And so it is with me. Because of video, I no longer must rely on the victim's creativity. I show them exactly what I want them to think. My use of video is ten times as important as my sole use of music. With my successful use of video, more specifically, the music video, my victims today even include some of the nicest teenage girls who now forfeit their virginity for the false images of cultural norms I display. My victims include as well the young man on the national honor society who brings a gun to school and murders his classmates to the surprise of many. Through video I glamorize violence. Through video I diminish the seriousness and special-ness of intimacy in relationships. I only show the casualness of sex, I don't show the consequences. My videos portray a material world, with no hard work or graphic disappointments. If a student does not know where to turn for a solution, I demonstrate wicked alter-natives in my video. All of the worlds' problems are solved in my three-minute mini-movies I masquerade as a simple and acceptable music video. After a few hours of conditioning, our now programmed young targets feel inclined to imitate the lifestyle the video suggested. They emulate the behavior, dress, language and look of their music video stars. The young ones have no idea they are playing with fire. Through decades of trial and error I've learned that the only way I can get a youth to fall into a treacherous pit is to first entice them into playing close to the edge. All I need there is just one slip and their future is ours. They painfully realize that the solitary lapse in decision-making and judgment today, creates con-sequences that last a *lifetime* tomorrow. And a *lifetime* is a long, long time, to be miserable. I accomplish this for you through my video false norms. All the women in videos are of the same size, beauty and attractiveness creating a false reality. The men are men only in name not in character. Instead of character and integrity I point to personality, appear-ance, and wealth as the exclusive determiners of attraction. The men and women on the videos are entertainers and make light of commitment, monogamy, and family. In essence they rob relationship of its' true value. I portray an importance on the emptiness of money, possessions and wealth, but I display only smiles and laughter. The students only see quick love, shallow relationships and a life of pleasure rather than the pursuit of wholeness and the struggle and reward of becom-ing one. My message through music, coupled with video imagery creates scenes in the eye of ones mind that can never be extinguished.

I teach girls how to dress, boys how to walk and talk, wanna-be gangsters how to kill, the young how to lie and deceive, and everyone else, simply how to live according to my standard— the rejection of that which is right. The funny thing is Master," Rebellion said with a laugh, "if I were to show up for dinner as I *really* am, I'd never make it past the welcome mat at the front door. But thanks to Deception and technology, I have the exquisite honor of being welcomed into almost every room of the house and every mind of the household. Some homes have either a television or radio in every room. I don't have to sneak in anymore, I'm allowed.

I can use the television, telephone, radio, satellites, tape players, cable, movies, and even newspaper. Through the use of satellite dishes the multitudes of works that I do throughout the world can now be received in the most remote, isolated homes. I once simply wrote those rural areas off as unreachable. Not anymore. I hold the keys to *every* house today. I come and go as I please. I even hold open the door to bring all of my wicked friends like Stubbornness, Ignorance, and Perversion, Ha! Ha Ha!" Rebellion giggled, "From ages two to ninety-two, my foothold is sure."

"As I said Master," spoke Deception, "because of this strong, talented fiend, the completion of our task draws nigh more easily."

"It sounds too good to be true!" exclaimed Satan. "Tell me of your successes."

"Hee, Hee, Hee Heeee! Success?" laughed Rebellion loudly. "I can take you to a house this instant with strong

Christian parents who loved and nurtured their young, gifted and talented son. He once potentially posed a dangerous risk to the dark side, but now due to our work with him, he's nothing more than an impotent, powerless pawn. While the parents pursued their careers I gladly stepped-in as his *mentor*. After school and home alone I offered him uncensored babysitting. He listened to whatever he wanted. And what did he want you may ask sir? He delighted in hardcore rap, a modern genre of urban music. Thug-life was his life of choice. He watched gangster rap videos to his hearts content. I engorged his life. I made it to his heart. He's trapped now, stone hard, pure rebellion. I, not long ago, called on my fruit to show itself in his life. And as expected this momma's boy recently brought unbelievable pain to many lives as a result of his murder of only one. Even though he knew right from wrong, he couldn't ignore my instruction nor escape the piercing of my talons into his wicked heart. Even though he's incarcerated for life, we have not stopped demanding fruit from his life. At the rate he's going in prison I anticipate seeing him here, among our ranks very soon, bringing others along with him. The voices of reason all fail to penetrate his calloused heart, no matter who the source. Mom tried, dad tried, the pastor tried they all tried to undo what I spent years getting done. I know another unusually gifted young girl destined once for greatness. But now my talons are so deep into her mind she refuses to honor the simplest act of obedience, being prompt for class. Daily late for school and class, sometimes she doesn't even bother to go. A habit my team created in her that no job, regardless of the pay or promise, can break. Her teachers, her mother and all those who reach out to her only meet her resistance. She even disrespected and fought her grandmother, how ridiculous. She blames her mother for the consequences of her rebellion. Her end you ask, but of course, perpetual unemployment. She'll never keep a job. She'll never be happy. Most importantly, she resists the teachings of The Holy…, I mean, *The Book*.

There's another who rebelled in dress, hairstyle and habits and foolishly longed for like-minded friends. He heard all of the warnings about drugs and alcohol. He made he pledges, signed the cards, and memorized the slogans. But his rebellious energy was irresistible when the opportunity came to take a drug called ecstasy. He did not know that that particular drug typically dehydrates internal organs. Moments after he popped his second pill, he fell suddenly into a deadly coma. Though he was only in the first quarter of his game of life, he exited the game without ever reaching his full potential or experiencing his true destiny. It happens all of the time; it's me, pure Rebellion!!"

Immediately a demon cried out, "THIS MASKED DEMON IS REBELLION!" The demons fluttered and hissed in jealous rage.

"Kill him!" they all yelled.

"Yeah, I crave some of his power!" shouted a demon from the crowd.

"Rip him up!" screeched a tiny imp.

Satan stood and whisked his hand through the air, sending rays of fire and sulfur from his fingers.

"Enough!" he said. "He, who conspires to come against

Rebellion, seals his own doom. I will not withhold the harshest of destructions for he who impedes Rebellion." Satan then turned to Rebellion and spoke softly, "Your work must go on! For he who is our greatest foe is not merely he who has received the truth, but he who has received and obeys. You my friend eliminate obedience, what a tremendous benefit to our work in the assault on the young. Deception then motioned to Rebellion to remove his cover. He revealed his face, hard as stone, black as the deep sea, and cold as the night.

Deception continued. "I'd like to introduce the rest of our team. But before I do, may summarize thus far? As you know, our final phase of manipulation and stimulation of the young seals their systematic destruction. Our purposes, adopted by the youth, provoke self-destruction and an eternal destiny with us. I am certain that as long as the church is limited in its infusion of youth, its progress will surely grow stale, irrelevant and eventually die in the cast of tradition. Without the vitality of the young, all movement of the church transforms into a monument rather than a mission. With our plan in full strength, even the youth presently in the churches, temples and cathedrals will fail to respond to the spirit and unction of the Lamb, thanks to the perfect horrid work of Rebellion."

Deception stood and leaned towards Satan to emphasize his next point. "In the strictest of confidence the intelligence command monitoring Rebellion's work informed me that in most instances Rebellion enjoys magnificent success. Rebellion averages three to four hours a day of conditioning through television, three to thirty hours a week of music video conditioning, eleven hours a week of conditioning through the telephone and a daily continuous barrage of at least 1,500-3,000 illicit, suggestive advertisements. In fact, $330 million a year Rebellion directs to alcohol advertising alone by the alcohol industry. As I compare all of this with only one to two hours of a frivolous stale worship experience per week, if that, our eventual dominance of our unsuspecting victims awaits only time. Our Enemy barely wins their attention. In fact, we've even adopted a few modified terms like, *"hell-a-vision"* instead of television. We think it more accurately describe its use."

"Amusing," said Satan. "Please continue your report."

"Just in case any students should happen to fall through the cracks, another recruit positioned to reinforce our doctrine of rebellion and anti-positive attitudes recently joined our team. Poised to execute his very powerful and exquisite work, this fine young specimen behind me explores further potential for perversion." Deception explained. "We call him WMD, our Weapon of Mass Destruction!"

Chapter 4

Deception motioned to the back of the room. The room suddenly fell silent as an awesome figure entered the room. He was smooth, with a physique as strong and fit as a statuesque warrior. He exhibited a warm, enticing, seductive smile. He casually, and with the utmost confidence, began his gait toward the front of the room. Every demon present began to howl, hiss and hoot. With each step, his muscles flexed and glistened in the faint light of the sulfuric abyss.

Abruptly, as he walked, he suddenly transformed into a stunning voluptuous woman right before everyone's eyes. She possessed exaggerated measurements, perfect symmetry and a curvaceous body. She had an irresistibly innocent, yet seductive countenance showing upon her face. The demonic jeering escalated into a lustful frenzy.

Without warning, the excitement in the lair shifted. Jeers and lustful hoots changed into ear piercing shrieks, for just as the "he" turned into a "she", the "she" turned into an "it". The "it" stood as a gruesome, slimy demon. Only four foot high, drooling from his contorted rotten mouth, panting with a sloppy tongue hanging through his crooked corroded fangs, the "it" looked purely hideous. Its hips rhythmically, without stopping, gyrated seductively, uncontrollably, and usually slow with intermittent quick jerks.

"GGGreetings, I am the crown prince, Spirit of LLLust!" he stuttered.

"No need to introduce yourself, Prince Lust. I have used you before. How will you help us in this time of need?" Satan asked.

Deception spoke up, "Your Nastiness, allow me please to explain the addition of this fine demon to the Teenage Task Force. This *thing* is one of our most tried and proven weapons. With his stuttering problem however we could be here all day if "he"...., I mean if "she"...., well if "it" were to explain."

"Very well Deception, state on," Satan commanded.

"We know sir, that any desire lacking restraint grows stronger each time it meets satisfaction. Where the focus goes, the power flows, you could say. We've also learned that as a man thinks, so he becomes."

"How do you know that?" asked Satan.

"Through research, sir, research," boasted Deception. "We unanimously decided that Lust best serves our need to feed the desires of sexuality so prevalent in the potent, sensitive, hormone-filled lives of the young. Once Lust entices the desires, our friend Temptation produces the bait and Rebellion then guarantees momentary satisfaction. Here's the catch, sir. The teenager soon begins to equate the "feeling" as something more than what it is. Namely, now get this, 'Love'!" Deception snickered, "Ha! Ha! And, why with all the ways in which we've polluted the notion of love, the teenage heart imminently lies at our virtual command. All for the sake of a feeling, which they think, is 'love'. You and I both know that mild or intense, infatuation is not true love."

"Please Deception; make your comments in reference to *true* love brief. I'd hate to have to jar your memory of how I detest the tenets of the other side," interrupted Satan.

"Yes, sir," said Deception.

"May I, I interject here?" whined Lust.

"You may," said Satan.

"I, I, I know no gender, sir. As you can see I am nnnnei-ther male nor ffffemale. I am LLLLust. Because of video and *hell-a-vision* and the mmmmusic, I ccccan promote any type of ssssexual desire I wwwwish among anyone. I have ssssuc-ceeded in many ssssuccessful ssssexual unions," Lust spit with a lisp. "Man and boy, girl to girl, ffffather and daughter, mother with sssson, ttteacher and student, coach and athlete, preacher and choir member, mayor and sssssecretary and sssso on. I have nnnno boundaries. I do not discriminate."

Deception excitedly added, "I've even seen wise, pro-fessional men dominated by an irresistible desire for inani-mate objects like shoes, women's clothes, whips and chains, nylons and an assortment of perversions all because of Lusts' tantalizing talons."

"What about the plan Lust, come on, get back to the plan for the young?" Satan demanded.

"The easiest combination of all, the easiest, sir, is the teenage boy and teenage girl union. RRRRebellion's input helps a ggggreat deal," stuttered Lust.

Deception jumped in, "Rebellion establishes 'the desire to do what one pleases' mode and reinforces its allegiance daily. In some cases teens prefer not to not to 'go all the way' but do so merely to spite mother and/or father. And we all know sexual intercourse outside of its intended purpose means destruction and estrangement from our Enemy. Like a fiery log out of the fireplace destroys, sex before or outside of marriage is deadly. And might I add the more teenagers develop into sexually active individuals, the more diseases and low self-esteem tramples their young hearts."

"What about our use of the condom lie, you must preserve its effectiveness?" reminded Satan.

"You *know* sir, that I, Deception, second only to you in the art of trickery, have attacked every effort to expose the condom lie. Some however, at the Centers for Disease Control, now suggest that doctors wear two pairs of latex gloves during surgical procedures for optimal protection against disease. Since these latex gloves are made of the same materials as the condoms, our team must work day and night to keep this information regarding this recent development from reaching the youth. Even the modestly alert teenager knows that a condom, only one sixth the thickness of a doctor's glove, hardly presents an adequate defense for the sexually transmitted diseases unleashed through the dark side. Even when one practices "safe sex", HIV infection enjoys a 25% chance of transmission. Besides, as long as condoms, protection and safe sex, draw all the headlines," he giggled, "our real target, the unprotected heart, eludes attention. An embittered, scarred heart takes decades to heal and without the proper attention, festers and eventually destroys itself and everyone around it."

Satan interjected sarcastically, *"Think they'll ever invent a condom for the heart?"* They all broke out in uncontrolled laughter.

Deception continued. "These to my left, sir, represent those working on our behalf as a result of Lust's extraordinary advantage." A host of determined demons stood. Among them were Rape, Falsehood, Cheating, Whoredom, Infidelity, Seduction, Pornography, Phone-sex, Child Abuse, Addiction, Broken-heartedness, Herpes, Syphilis, Gonorrhea, Fantasy Sex, HIV Infection, Flirtation, Homosexuality, Perversion, Divorce, Depression and Discouragement. "Lust's devices annihilate so many lives, so many families, and such an incredible host of clergy we simply refer to him as WMD, the weapon that brings mass destruction. The younger Lust begins, the greater our success rate. Lately a new and surprise resource, the World Wide Web, brings us our broadest and most expansive touch, the Internet. Before the Internet our first pornography exposure with a student did not happen until their 11th year of life. But now with the onslaught of the Internet, our average first opportunity to sow pornographic seeds occurs at 5 years old. There's more to say on that later."

CHAPTER 5

Deception asked Lust to be seated. He then turned to Satan and spoke enthusiastically. "Accomplishing your desire of destroying the *will to win* of the young appears on the horizon now sir," Deception said admiringly. "But sir, if you don't mind me asking, with your power so intimidating and real, and your grip so strong and tentacles so deep into the hearts of so many, why must the *will* of the young remain so important to you?"

"Must I forever labor with your lack of understanding?" Satan blurted at Deception with disappointment. "Follow closely as I explain. You just may learn a thing or two. I happen to know a few things myself about our Enemy. He adores praise; not artificially yielded praise but sincere unprovoked praise. He inhabits praise. He dwells among and sits upon the praises of these underlings. He honors praise, but never forces it, not ever. He loves these despicable imperfect creatures so much it's sickening. He's content in loving them until they simply love Him back, particularly the little ones. But they must *choose* to love Him. Therein lies our purpose. I purposely hit Him where it hurts...the love of His life, His creation! If everything He does and has done supports and establishes humankind, everything that we do must confuse and destroy humankind. If He uses love, we must use hate.

He's their *heavenly father*, and with them they make a happy family; I am his home-wrecker. In heaping defeat after defeat after defeat upon His faithful, relentlessly, soon they'll simply give up, give in, and stop *choosing* His way. Some will even blame him instead of me causing me added delight. I'm enjoying great success of course, but my work must go on. I will not stop. We will not stop, until His heart bleeds generations of grief, and His creatures, destined for despair reap their just destructions. Thus, we choose the young. And yes, I want their *will*, their freedom to *choose*. I endeavor to imprison them in habits so controlling that they uncontrollably begin to choose me," Satan said through a wide grin. "So continue Deception, tell me of your help for me in influencing their will?"

"Beginning with the teenage boy, through the use of pornography and sexually explicit X-rated and R-rated movies, our Task Force first creates an obsession in the battlefield, the mind. We make every young girl his desire, or if necessary, his victim. To accomplish our goals, we manipulate him to speak lies with eyes sincere as a newborn babe. "You know I love you, baby", he'll say. "If you love me too you'll show me," that's another one. Of course this will be only until that dreadful moment of pleasure is reached, when lust is satisfied. And if he can't get what he wants, we'll teach him basically how to *take* it. So obedient to the voice of Lust, his eyes will survey and undress each female he sees, further driving the talons of Lust deep into his heart.

Shameful behaviors he once avoided like phone-sex, date rape, voyeurism, and girl watching soon all end up as norms in his life. Our agenda replaces his life call and perversion becomes part of the fabric of his character. If he does happen to marry one day, Satan forbid, his mind, already experienced with a multiplicity of fantasy lovers, imaginary partners, one-night-stands and one-time affairs, prohibits the possibility of monogamy and fidelity. His young bride will fail to compete with the pornographic perfection he's entertained in his imagination. His frustrations soon will manifest themselves in abuse. Unable to surpass the imagined lovers of his mind, his wife will suffer from his unfair expectations. His verbal abuse will extinguish her love and their passion. Our nature will reveal itself in his every action, his every thought and his every attitude. A young man stripped of his ability to think and to act on his own, denotes a demoralized man, less than a man, the shell of a man.

And as for the will of the young woman, once robbed of her virginity, each act of sex out of wedlock represents to us an act of violence against the will of the Lord of Hosts. Sex becomes a kind of emotional violence that shatters the frail integrity of the teenage heart. Lord Peer Pressure stands ready and committed to attend *every* date, *every* home visit, and *every* phone conversation with her love interest to encourage defeat, *every* time. With her dates *pressuring* her physically toward sex, and her friends *pressuring* her socially toward sex, the media provides that chord of reinforcement needed to convince her that she's finally *ready* for sex. The media convinces the young women of our perennial lie, that she's missing out on sex because 'everyone else is doing it', although most are not. Soon she'll surely tire and then yield her body to us. Our decision, our lies, but it's *her* consequences, leaving *her* heart marred forever, and unable to truly love.

All other sins are outside of the body but they that sin for us sexually, sin against their own bodies. And of course, in due time, our most valuable weapon for these misled young girls obtains its prime opportunity to visit, Princess Abortion. We make Princess Abortion appear at first logical and attractive, but in the end she is a devastating, ruthless comrade. As you know, she's the twin sister of Murder. The emotional consequences can be life-long for the young lady. Most females probably don't even know that the possession of personal value and honor ranks second to only life itself in the hierarchy of worth. If it is not in its intended marital use, every act of sex, whether true love, infatuation, or some other deviance, plucks away from one's honor and worthiness. Princess Abortion, whom we affectionately nicknamed, '*Quick- fix Cutie*', QC for short', dishonors the Enemy's creation. Self esteem then fades. Each compromise or sexual encounter, whether traditional or oral, symbolizes for the young woman a single petal ripped from a rose. After multiple compromises, our female teen victims resemble a diseased barren stem. Although once a fresh, beautiful, fragrant rose capable of years of growth, blossoms and beauty, she's now just an empty stem, raped of its splendor, significance and awe. Some men boast of their sexual "conquests". And of course, some boys pride themselves on creating this "stem" condition, although the thought of marrying one would never survive a moment's consideration. A real man desires a rose. How delicious!" smiled Deception, "oh how delicious."

"May I ask you a question Deception?" Satan interjected.

"Yes sir, please," responded Deception.

"You mentioned, very briefly, about the work of Princess Abortion "QC" as you call her... and that the emotional consequences of Abortion 'can' be life-long. I am curious, if one of our key weapons against young girls belongs to Abortion, why then does your statement suggest that complete success may elude Abortion?"

"As I suggested sir, Abortion completes in an instant that glorious feat which takes us sometimes decades to accomplish, murder. In that regard, Abortion is key, very key. Our diversion tactics insure the longevity for so-called *safe legal abortions*. That's a play on words, is it not? Abortion is never *safe* and according to our Enemy's economy it is always *illegal*. And as long as the debate in this region is centered on our diversionary issue, *choice*, the real issues, money, selfishness, and the destruction of life, never entertain any serious talk or discussion. With approximately 4,000 B.E.E.'s, that is, Baby Elimination Executions daily, at the rate of $300 to $450 each, our abortionists enjoy at last check, at least 1.2 million dollars daily. Legal murder for hire, the fruit of "pro-choice", I know you love that phrase your nastiness. Now that's a billion-dollar industry. Thanks to Abortion we've masterfully arranged to plague the heart of the Enemy with great grief. As an added delight, the number of teenage girls committing suicide on or around the anniversary of their abortions provokes an unfathomable sweet taste , like icing on the cake. However, as in this case and many cases, both new and some old, but some not so..."

"DECEPTION!" Satan jumped in. "I find it unnerving how you avoid answering my question. My patience with your stammering and figuring grows thin," Satan shouted. "Get to the point. Speak clearly. Why did you report that the emotional consequences of abortion *can* be life long? What impedes the complete dominance of abortion?"

Deception paused in silence. "Promise number 2,029", uttered Deception with concern ducking as if he knew another smack was coming.

"What is promise 2,029?" Satan mimicked, speaking in Deceptions voice.

"Let the record show," Deception began, "that I *reluctantly* remind you of promise number 2,029. Just remember you asked me to tell you. Recorded in the first letter written by John, section one paragraph nine I first read these words." Deception took a step back knowing Satan would scowl at the quote now forming in his mouth for delivery. "If we confess our sins He is faithful and just to forgive us our sins, and to cleanse us from *all* unrighteousness," Deception blurted. Satan appeared calm at first, then ENRAGED! He transformed into a ghastly creature five times his own size and let out a piercing shriek that lasted almost sixty seconds. It riveted the foundations of the dark side.

"I HATE THAT BOOK," he shouted. "I hate it! I hate it. I hate it. I HATE IT WITH A PERFECT HATRED," he added. "PROCRASTINATION! FORGETFULNESS! Front and center," he demanded. Two very similar demons limped and scampered to the front. They were used to each other because they worked so often as a team. "I want you Procrastination, to make sure that these young ones put off and put off and put off the reading of *The Book*. Do whatever it takes. I don't care just make it happen. And you, Forgetfulness, hide from their memory, the thought to read. Fight with willful abandon any attempt to commit to memory any words or any phrases or any paragraphs from that detestable book. You *must* keep it from their memory, understood?"

"Yes sir," they saluted in unison.

"Very well, for they must forget to read repeatedly," Satan mumbled.

"I'll do the best I can," said Forgetfulness. "But may I solicit some assistance?" he asked.

"Can't you handle this assignment, Forgetfulness?" Satan asked.

"What assignment....oh...yes the assignment. The task, sir, the task is not the problem. It's just that once when I was alone I nearly perished because of the Spirit of the Lamb. It seems as though no matter how deeply I bury or hide elements of *The Book* in the dark caverns of the mind, the Spirit of the Lamb can resurrect these sayings and references even without a request from our victim. If I begin to resist this clever move, I then become the hunted. And when I retreat, the appropriate saying, relevant to the need, is then escorted promptly to the front of the memory at a moment's notice."

"You may get help demon, but if you fail in warring against the Spirit, then we must simply inhibit the promises from ever taking root." Satan then yelled, "Distraction!" A quick, jittery spirit bounded to the front with nervous energy. His wandering eyes shared a preoccupation with everything other than his conversation with Satan. His attention span, no longer than a moment or two failed to grasp any one thought without bounding inexplicably to the next.

"Yes sir," he said quickly.

"I want you to...," Satan started. Distraction had noticed a large fly buzzing about the head of a demon not far behind him. After careful aim, he snapped his tongue and consumed the fly, which was more than four feet away. "DISTRACTION!" Satan said, "PAY ATTENTION! Your *life* depends on it!" Satan resumed stating his desire. "You must monitor the preacher, the teacher, the youth minister, and anyone else who teaches the tenets of *The Book* to the young. Whenever or wherever someone speaks a promise, immediately distract all attention away from it. Use whatever's available to you. A flirtatious wink, traffic to the restroom, an inconsiderate conversation, a baby crying, a wandering thought, the passing of a note, gossiping in church, even the clipping of fingernails all serve as acceptable modes of effective distraction. A ringing cell phone works, as well as a microphone whining, or even a light that flickers. Do whatever you can to distract the promises that come forth from *The Book*. The promises of *The Book* must not, CANNOT become common knowledge for any of our young simple victims."

CHAPTER 6

Deception raised his talon to speak.

"Speak, Deception," Satan said.

"I'd like to introduce are final member of our Teenage Task Force before we visit our victims." Deception turned toward the back of the room and nodded his head. Through the rear doors burst an angry unruly demon, strong and destructive. Instead of walking around chairs and tables and clusters of demons, he walked right through them. He broke chairs, smacked demons, crushed tables and growled. His muscles and veins bulged from his neck, face...everywhere! His beady, red, blood-shot eyes pierced the room. Wimpy demons scattered as he appeared and approached Satan's throne.

"Wise choice, Deception," remarked Satan. "The Duke of Violence, my personal favorite supporter of anti-social behavior. How will you support the mission of the Teenage Task Force, Duke of Violence?"

"Simple," said Violence, in a fierce, husky voice. "Most youth possess an innate sense of powerlessness. The grown-ups make the rules and rule the game. The grown-ups make the decisions. The grown-ups know what's 'best'. I can change all of that with just a small taste of violent destruction. Through me the powerless transform into the powerful. Give me an insignificant harmless teenage pip-squeak, put a gun in his hand, and instantaneously I'll convert him into a violent killer, a 'big man'. I fill the heads of teenagers with my voice. I speak boastings he's never heard before. I'll build him up. I'll put him in charge, feeding his ego and esteem all the way."

"What makes you so certain of success?" asked Satan.

"Well, to begin with, it worked 511 times last year in the Nation's capital, 511 dead young people. Most of them were young men between the ages of 16 and 25. Secondly, I provide the platform for continuous violence among the youth through structured elaborate gang activity. It never stops. Third, as with any great fruitfulness, rotten or righteous, growth requires seed. A little seed yields a little harvest. Much seed yields much harvest. And if you, dear sir, desire to captivate the youth, destroy them and even use them to destroy others, the seed planted MUST be nourished. And *my* seed and nourishment plan, huh, huh, huh, huh, dear sir, by the time a student reaches the twelfth grade they will have witnessed over 200,000 acts of violence, 25,000 of them, violent murders. All digested while sitting in a vegetative, passive TV-watching-state. By the time a student graduates from high school their home, most likely headed by a single parent, in reality becomes my classroom. In most of those homes, the single parent, statistically a mom working at least one or two jobs, comes home too exhausted for parenting. So who do you think raises the children? Huh, huh huh…ME!" Violence chuckled in amusement.

"More effective than the passive conditioning, my newest tiller of the fertile garden of the battlefield, interactive video, remains unmatched in effectiveness and efficiency in conditioning young teens. You know them sir, Battle Star, Game Station, Rude Boy, Karaté King; my expertise in this category advances my seed planting process to an art. The mind then takes these interactive video seeds and convinces one's emotion that one is actually committing the violence when playing these games. The mind is so convincing, in many cases the body doesn't even know what is real or fake. When shooting on the video game, the *mind* is actually *shooting*. When killing on the game, the *mind* is actually *killing*. Through interactive video there is blood spilled and gunshots fired but no consequences only amusement. Violence is accepted. Most importantly students become desensitized to the dark side. I plant gruesome thoughts, dark side plots and evil harm schemes sometimes only with the help of these games. Through sound effects, visualization, hand controls and interaction, I can lock onto the student's intellect, time and attention for HOURS without ever being noticed. With the help of Lady Addiction, my interactive video game takes precedence over food, employment and even relationship. The physiological responses to the simulated violence and its excitement prove my effectiveness here. The euphoric feeling produced by the release of hormones of ecstasy in the mind is consistent with the neurological responses to a cocaine high. Playing my video game just once is not good enough. The excitement causes repeated involvement creating symptoms similar to drug addiction behavior."

"First amusement then addiction, I must say I like your style Violence." Satan said sounding impressed.

Violence continued. "To the teenager, the game only provides a few hours of entertainment, but to me and for our purposes, the interactive video game is not a game, but an invaluable, indispensable sower of the seeds of destruction, familiarizing the heart with the darkest evils. Of all your lessons Satan, your teaching on patience sticks most vividly in my mind. So with these, it may take some time, I know. For some it takes two years, others five, some ten years, but sooner or later the seeds of violence produce certain devastation. And I'm willing to wait."

"And opposition?" Satan inquired.

"Our opposition is quite limited, sir. Most parents caught up in the hustle and bustle of their own little worlds of money, materialism and careers, leave their children raising themselves. Children come home from school to an empty house, cook for themselves and find ways to satisfy all of their emotional needs themselves. I spend more time with students, than most parents. The average father's daily seven minutes of one on one time hardly compares to the two to fours of *my* daily, uninterrupted true devotion.

The students' standard for personal approval eventually becomes peer approval. Their friends double as their family and in many cases their *gang*. And what's wrong with three or more harmless teenagers bonding together? Nothing's wrong with that actuality. But plant the seeds of destruction and power, take away healthy alternatives, add a little boredom and eventually I gain the victory. I guarantee I'll find a way to entice their young silly minds to accomplish MY goals. Oh how wonderfully disappointed the Enemy will be!"

Violence snickered. "A harmless group of boys, playing rough with another harmless group of boys is not very useful to me or for us. In fact it's normal. Have one boy from one group commit an act of violence against another or in some way disrespect another, then encourage retaliation, and I assure you that Prince Murder, that lovable creature, proves himself time and time again. In fact, the current language includes my name I believe they call it 'Gang Violence', how cute?" remarked Violence.

"Thank you Violence for your report," Satan said.

"There's more, sir," Violence stated proudly.

"More? Please continue," Satan responded stirred.

"I have a secret weapon. Well it's not much of a secret. It helps a great deal though. My long-time friend, Sir Delusion, upon my request, committed to ensure the prevalence of mind and mood altering drugs and chemicals. We develop improper drug use strategies here and apply them to deviations of drugs mostly engineered and concocted through our laboratories. Their representatives stand there against the side wall." A naughty crew of grim anxious demons snapped to attention along the adjacent wall. One by one they identified their domains; "Hallucinogen", "Alcohol", "Nicotine", "Heroin", "Amphetamine", "Cocaine", the role call echoed. The last seemed most unbearable than all, she identified herself as Lady Addiction.

"Please Violence, tell me, do your friends work as diligently as you? Explain the relationship between you and these seductive associates," Satan prodded.

"Kindly sir," Violence obliged. I'd like to reiterate that

these helpful badly behaved acquaintances need not be present for me to do my work but they make it much, much easier. Under the influence of alcohol, let's say, even one twelve-ounce dosage, I, Violence, become quite attractive. Add a few more beers, I become even irresistible. In over-indulgence, however, my propensity to destroy not only my victim, but his or her associates, friend, foe, or relative increases exponentially. Beer, liquor, joints, blunts and cigarettes represent only the foretaste, excuse the pun, of manipulation and bondage. Inspired to master chemical and other drug abuse, Delusion and I launched wicked combinations that spike drug and alcohol effectiveness. If I take one drug and pervert it with another substance, intensified intoxication abounds. Or in some cases my presentation of a drug in a different form produces a greater ecstatic experience. Okay, okay…I must give credit to whom credit is due. These last two inspiring bright ideas originated with Lady Addiction. Her inescapable grip tightens fastest in chemical and drug mixing or varied form use. For example, for years drugs were only taken orally. But if you change its form, the same drug can now be smoked or injected for greater access to the blood stream and greater addiction. One liquor may cause inebriation, but when mixed with another and consumed its toxic levels zoom upward hastening my irresistibility. With these tactics and these friends around, and drug-contaminated thinking, inhibitions and the power to say no to me, simply evaporate."

"I need help demon, show me concrete ways in which your strategy strengthens the enterprise of the Teenage Task

Force." Satan asked.

"With pleasure, sir," Violence shot back. "Last year alone, over 660,000 cases of purely violent date-rapes occurred, unreported. Of those cases approximately 80% of the time alcohol coursed through the veins of the young man. In fact, though she yelled *no*, the alcohol in his blood interpreted her *no* as a *yes* in his intoxicated ear. Whether she screamed NO, kicked NO, or scratched NO, a resounding YES is all the alcohol ever allows the boy to hear. Many of the unwanted pregnancies that end in abortion begin this way, as does the communication of herpes, and HIV infection. Young women who ignore their own common sense only to join these same young men in consumption of alcohol astound even me. Teenage logic...I don't completely understand it, I just manipulate it.

These colleagues of mine are to me what gasoline is to fire. Teenage boys with their macho levels of bravado and testosterone, become helplessly under my control, explosive if I wish. I cannot fail in encouraging their self-destruction. Normally because of my strong seduction, I can guarantee arrest and incarceration, expulsion from school, bad reputation, or even what's most helpful PGR, *Perpetual Gang Retaliation*. And what's more, I'm seeing teenage girls compromising in this area nearly as much as boys."

"Define, if you will, this PGR?" Satan asked with interest. "Modern terms and abbreviations get rather confusing to me."

"PGR...is an unending cycle of blind, senseless violence against friend or foe, which devastates community moral. In others when you think it's over, it's not over. It could be random or intentional. I can make boys, once childhood playmates, gun one another down as teenagers. I can also make two girls, once high school best friends; stab one another at a gang leaders command. I have even made brothers and sisters kill their mother and or father just because they interfered with their *crew*. I plant the seeds; they pull the trigger, and you, master gain the victory. How brutal! How cruel! HOW PERFECTLY VIOLENT!"

CHAPTER 7

"Your preparation Deception impresses me. In fact, this plan excites me more now than ever before," Satan said. "I'd like to make just a few things perfectly clear. I expect all of you to be on your job daily. Maintain faithfulness to the second, not only the hour. Not one moment, nay, even an instant can go unused. No student can go undisturbed, undirected, nor must we accept, unhindered exposure to the Lamb. Not one, hear me, not one student lives without my influence. My touch must saturate their worlds undetected. To demonstrate my commitment to this mission, if need be, I'll freely eliminate anyone on this Task Force found slacking on his or her assignment. You know me; I'll destroy you first then ask questions later. There's always some other worthy demon prepared to fill vacancies. With your indulgence, Lord Deception I'd like to ask once again," Satan paused, "please disclose any and all risks of this operation to my kingdom of darkness? Even the slightest setback unexpected, retards our progress for generations. We must be prepared!"

Deception stumbled over his words knowing the inadvertent truth he discovered during the most intense phase of his research. He knew this information would have to come out sooner or later. Taking a long, deliberate deep breath, he started speaking shyly, reluctantly, in a low tone.

"Sir, you know according to *The Book* that the effectual fervent prayer of the righteous makes a difference."

"I am uncomfortably aware, proceed," Satan said irritably.

"Many of these teenagers, though not churched themselves, live with mothers, fathers, grandmothers, brothers and/or sisters faithfully praying for them."

"Yes…and…so what! You made me to understand that with a well thought-out plan like ours, as you ascertain, even prayer would be ineffective," Satan remarked.

"Yes, that's…uh… partially true sir, yes. But if exposed to prayer cover, our victims quite possibly may recognize our assaults as opportunities for growth and maturity. Some of the verbiage in *The Book*, somewhere in the letter written by James and the first section, our Enemy suggests the difficulties we unleash and the hardships we present may actually be cause to rejoice. It goes on to recommend that the reader should 'consider it joy' when the tests come. The prayer stuff uncovers things…uh…kind of, sort of…. If they know that which is tried in the fire comes out stronger and purer, our young victims may respond, lets say, *differently*."

"Ah! But what if the victims succumb as planned?" Satan asked. "What if a student utterly fails under our combined badgering?"

Deception now sweating profusely and a little agitated reluctantly responded, "There remains still a small, small possibility of redemption," said Deception. He held up his thumb and forefinger approximating about an inch, emphasizing his point.

"UGH! You are beginning to annoy me! Are you saying that if we give all that we've got, the best of the power of the dark side, and if, per chance, we succeed, and our victims succumb to our plot, somewhere in the great unknown a minuscule possibility of redemption exists?" Satan asked wailing his arms mockingly. "Exactly how *slight* would this be?"

"Well sir, my estimation…." Deception hesitantly continued.

"WOULD YOU SPEAK DEMON!" shouted Satan causing Deception to jump almost out of his scaly skin.

"Yes sir." There was a long pause. Then Deception took another deep breath and said, "Okay…I figure about…a…one hundred percent chance of redemption, give or take a percent or so," he creaked in a blurt.

"WHAT? ONE HUNDRED PERCENT CHANCE OF REDEMPTION? How can this be?" Satan let on. He knew the answer. Deception refused to reply. "I said, HOW! Do you hear me? HOW?" Satan insisted standing and screaming at the top of his rotten lungs as if he didn't know.

"I don't know," Deception lied

"HOW DEMON? Satan insisted.

"I said I don't know!" Deception said refusing to give the answer.

Satan then grabbed Deception by the throat with one clutch of his wicked fist while drawing back the other threatening another punch. "FOR THE LAST TIME, DEMON, HOW CAN THIS BE?"

"Because of the **CROOOOSSSSSSS!**" Deception cried out, like a confessing murderer no longer able to take the interrogation of the skilled detective. *"BECAUSE OF THE CROSS, ANYONE, AT ANYTIME, ANYWHERE, CAN BE REDEEMED."* Deception blurted in defeat. "There has never been a record anywhere in history of the discovery of the body of the one we crucified. We cannot hide that truth", Deception confessed.

A hush came over the room. No demon anywhere dare peep or hiss. Silence permeated the dark side. Satan stood perfectly still. He stood silent at his throne of brimstone, almost as if in a trance or daydream. Fear gripped every fallen angel in the room. No one knew what to expect from Satan in response to this looming revelation. Like a recurring nightmare or the repetition of a broken record, Satan's mind began to replay over and over again Jesus' exclamation at the cross. Satan thought his reign was beginning but Jesus announced instead:

"It...is...finished!" Then again Satan heard those words "It...is...finished!" And then much more intensely they rang in his ear, "IT...IS...FINISHED!" Those words plagued Satan every day since they first pierced his darkness. Jesus should have said, "I am finished", but instead he used the word "it" as if there was a mission about to be launched and the cross was the only prerequisite. It was because of those words that Satan could not sleep. He could still, after two-thousand years, hear Jesus' voice, see his ultimate sacrifice and sense the unmatched power of that unconditional love on that now regrettable Calvary afternoon. The supreme power that brought Jesus back to life and out of the grave was a power with which Satan could not contend. Had he known of the resurrection miracle to follow, he would never have nailed Jesus to the tree, he presumed. Of course that was pure conjecture.

"Ah! The Cross," he began breaking the silence. "My first and unparalleled defeat of the Nazarene," he claimed falsely. "Second in excellence only to my imminent dominance of his spineless kingdom," he misleadingly proclaimed. "I took his power that day! You see it today, don't you Deception?" Satan said pleadingly desperate for approval. "You see it in my pattern of success with his most elect. I defeated him that day, and, and, our Enemy knows it! Once I destroy the next generation, the future generations shall serve me as well! Come Deception, the time has come. Let us check our progress."

Every demon knew Jesus was alive. Jesus suffered the crucifixion high on a hill lifted up. All men and demons saw him crucified. And just as he predicted, three days later he arose. At the crucifixion it was typical to wrestle the hands of the crucified to the cross in preparing for the entry of the driven spike. But when Jesus came to be crucified there was no wrestling, his arms were already stretched wide, he said, "No man take my life, I lay it down, to redeem". Jesus overcame Satan's greatest strike, the blow of death. Jesus is alive. None of Satan's "explanations" were compelling. Fear and trickery were his tactics. He bullied his demons into believing that he would rule in the end. Short-lived success gave empty confidence. Satan continued his masquerade. Now the Teenage Task Force proceeded to press their plan onward. The assignments now made, the demons now in place, and the youth of the world targeted for elimination, Deception led his team to war.

CHAPTER 8

Months earlier, Deception identified four teens from four different communities representing four unique challenges for the Teenage Task Force. Lust, Rebellion, Corruption and others commenced their advancements on all fronts. The Teenage Task Force chose four *normal* unsuspecting youths as subjects for their plan. Abounding in peculiarities, as most teenagers do, these four also possessed common distinctions that unite the vast majority of students their age. They each enjoyed few close friends and feared typical foes. They each shared the propensity to tease and reasons to each suffer teasing. They each experienced very different relationships with their parents as well as different ways in which they responded to those relationships. As a result of the influence of modern culture, they each maintained a heightened awareness of their sexuality or lack thereof, and a keen awareness of peer pressure. Though seemingly innocent they also each represented a frightening threat to the kingdom of darkness. Not so much because of who they are, or what they possess. Not because of their influence or relations, but because of their resemblance. "Let us make man in our own image according to our likeness," Genesis chapter one reads. This truth served as a perennial thorn in Satan's flesh. The very thought that He who Lucifer once aspired to dethrone had the audacity to create and replenish the earth with creatures of His holy *likeness* and image. It was upsetting for the Prince of Darkness. 'In His own image', these youth and all of humankind belonged in this category. Resembling the Holy One proved to be Satan's dreadful and timeless reminder of the potential of each of his victims. Satan knew that faith as insignificant in size as a mustard seed could usher generational change through any one of God's creations.

So the Teenage Task Force chose James, Sandy, Ronnie and Leah. James overflowed with giftedness. Most teenagers possess at least some talents. Talents attract attention and open doors of opportunity, but giftedness denotes a specific ability. Gifts once given, are without repentance, that is to say they never return to the giver and creator. They are the blessing of the possessor eternally. James' gift was his brilliance. He produced extraordinary and creative ideas. His personality exhibited an exciting magnetism. He effortlessly influenced others. Often, after casual conversations with friends or classmates, the aftertaste of his presence would convince anyone of his special-ness. But somehow he allowed his special–ness to disappear behind a cloud of constant compromise.

Deception explained to Satan, "I present to you James, your ugliness. Thanks to my personal attention to this poor child, he lives convinced that he does not belong, and that he exists only as a social misfit. So oppressively overwhelmed with greatness, the seduction of the mediocrity around him mesmerizes him. I hate to brag sir, but because of my superb use of trickery this youngster believes that life as an African American devoid of the ability to entertain or compete athletically, invalidates his ethnic origin and authenticity. An amusing lie is it not? He constantly seeks validation by acting *hard*, or disturbing his class or trying to be funny. He even boasts of foolish things, one day even brandishing a gun he brought to school. These actions reveal a classic desperation to fit-in. I did discover several of the plans prepared for him by the Enemy. I didn't get all of the information, but my sources confirm that potentially hundreds of thousands of others of low income status will experience unlimited business opportunities in their field of work because of James' innovative ideas."

"How do you know these things? Even I can't see into the future," Satan asked with skepticism in his voice.

"Neither can I, nor any of these demons. But eavesdropping can be particularly helpful. Several years ago as one of your legions monitored his prayer, something startling happened. James completed a drawing that evening, not of a house, apartment or an office building. But he constructed, on two pieces of paper taped together, an entire community. He prayed that night to be able to accomplish the same thing as an adult, or as he put it, "when I grow up."

"So what makes you so sure Deception that this little boy's empty wish will come true?" asked Satan.

"That's just it, Sir. Though we thought of it as an empty wish, James' empty wish caught the careful ear of our Enemy that night. Our reliable sources again confirm that our Enemy granted that prayer that night, at that moment. He charged His angels to deliver it at what He called the *Appointed Time*. Our prayer monitors report today that angels have been whispering James's little prayer after all of these years into the ear of the Enemy."

"Are you so weak as to not defeat these angels? You defeated them in the past demon, so why worry?" asked Satan.

"Sir, sorry to correct you again but we've never actually defeated the angels of the Lord of Hosts, We've detained them, yes, but never defeated them. As far as the *Appointed Time* is concerned we are not permitted to touch the *Appointed Time*. The best we can do is hope that at the *Appointed Time*, our victim, due to disobedience and compromise, ends up outside the will of his creator."

Satan interrupted. "You mean that if Rebellion succeeds with the student, the student then forfeits his destiny before it arrives," Satan surmised.

"Exactly sir," responded Deception. "Perhaps at the so called *Appointed Time* we find our young victim already expelled from school, incarcerated, or simply giving up on school and dropping out."

"What specifically did the Bishop of Souls grant that night?" asked Satan.

"Well again, we don't have any concrete proof, but our reports indicate that James has the potential and is, or was, destined to be one of the most unique African-American architectural consultants of the new millennium. His success would set a new precedent and open the doors for others." Deception stated.

"Ha, ha, ha, ha," Satan laughed. "This introverted, follow-the-crowd child, an architect? Insane!"

"No sir, it's not insane with promise number 708 on

record," responded Deception. Satan smiled, and then his smile turned into a grimace.

"What, pray tell, is promise number 708?"

"I regretfully report that the book of Numbers section 23, paragraph 19 indicates, 'God is not a man that He should lie; nor the son of man that He should change His mind. If He said it shall He not do it? If He promised it, shall He not make it good?'"

Satan knew too well that just as he and his demons strategize and scheme, the Lord of Hosts intricately prepares what the average person might call *coincidences*. The omniscient one used small miracles masquerading as coincidences where He preferred to remain anonymous. Satan was much more forceful in his approach to seduce young lives. The Holy One simply loved the students and provided opportunities for them to *choose* the Light. This angered the wicked one. So pure, so truthful, so holy was his enemy.

"Blasted!" shrieked Satan. "Promises, promises, remind me Deception, to appoint enforcers to encourage the work of Forgetfulness and Procrastination the moment we return. We must not fail in the promotion of biblical ignorance."

CHAPTER 9

Sandy stood in the mirror, primping her hair. She just couldn't seem to get it right. Although her mother disapproved of the make-up she liked to wear, Sandy double-checked her purse before leaving for school, making sure her cosmetics remained hidden but accessible. It only took a few moments in the bathroom mirror before school, to "put on her face", lipstick, blush, eyeliner and eye shadow. Sandy did not enjoy the same popularity as did most of her friends. A lying spirit kept her convinced that she did not possess the same beauty either.

Deception said, "Sir Nasty, our plans for Sandy astound even me. She's not a bad child; she just needs some attention. The Spirit of Lust found and groomed just the right young man for her, the right someone who'll give her the right attention, affection and say all the right things. He is also going to give her something else to remember him by for the rest of her miserable life." Lust aimed not only at satisfaction but earnestly endeavored for contamination as well. "Her mother though, causes us great concern", Deception added.

"Ah yes," Satan cut off Deception, "If this Sandy is the daughter of the woman I'm thinking of, at 2505 Lake Avenue, I do know her mother, and I know her quite well."

"Is it true, sir, that she is not only an Agent, but a Warrior?"

"A Warrior of the highest order, she is an Intercessory Prayer Warrior. Not only did we war with her before, thousands fell by the weapons of her warfare. You should've known this!" Satan insisted.

"When picking our target students we did consider her mother's fabled history with us, actually. But don't warriors deserve out attention too?" Deception responded.

"I guess that is true", Satan reluctantly agreed. "Well anyway, what kind of relationship does this mother have with our victim?" Satan asked.

"Not bad sir, but our thorough preparation ensures success. Rebellion has informed us that he can teach Sandy to rebel against the standards instilled by her mother…that is of course if Lust can make his connection through our boy whom he's completely dominating. Once estranged from her mother, used and abused by her boyfriend, and betrayed by her girlfriends, she'll be all alone. Ah, such sweet solitude. Once all alone, we'll unleash a barrage of indefensible attacks on her battlefield."

"Detail, demon, Give me details!" Satan said impatiently.

"Certainly, Master of Crookedness, first we'll revisit notions of how unattractive she is in comparison to what we repeatedly refer to as *everyone else*. Our constant taunts and accusations of 'fat', 'ugly' and 'undesirable' will pummel her self-esteem. Our insinuations distort even the obvious beauty she sees in the mirror. Our famous lie, "your father left your mother because of you", already establishes a platform of rejection. Secondly, her repeated acts of love-less sex gives us grounds for daily jolts of that worthless, devalued, dishonored feeling. Finally, with her smile continually upside down, we'll convey every minor disappointment in her life as a seemingly insurmountable mountain we call rejection. From there we costume everything that goes wrong in her life as a personal form of rejection and rebuke. Isolated, hit by these tried and true assaults, no youth can survive. She'll be so calloused, hard, and full of murmuring and complaining we could better describe her as our living vile of poison. Sandy's disposition will eventually infect people and programs wherever she goes. Who wants to be around a personality as sour as that everyday? No one does!"

"What is the current status of Lust and the boy?" Satan demanded.

"Sex and Perversion saturate the life of the boy, thanks to the superb work of our team member Prince Lust! In addition, Pornographic literature, late night *hell-o-vision*, and sensuous music videos are his daily addictive diet. When he surfs the Internet he exposes himself to a 24 hour buffet of over 400,000 adult book stores and peepshows, that don't even check his I.D. *All you can eat* wickedness. We call this practice, Corruption Consumptions, or CC's for short. We get 3.5 hours of CC's 7 days a week. He lands an average 2,000 to 5,000 hits weekly on explicit adult sexual content sites. Our pornographic literature and websites specialize in every possible fetish and attraction in order to etch graphic displays of debauchery on his mind. He lives to watch and record raw, uncut, lewd music videos. His appetite for the bikini clad video girls and dance club exotics grows deeper and more addictive each day."

"What kind of interference do you get from his mother and father?" Satan asked.

"Interference? Pssshaw! On the contrary, the question is…where would we be without the enablement of his parents?" Deception shot back. "His naïve parents, following our lead, get him whatever he wants. They think the 'things' they buy can replace the 'time' they should be spending with him. They act more like his peers than his parents. He has the latest and fastest computer and a big DO NOT DISTURB sign on his bedroom door. He even, now get this, put a lock on his bedroom door. His parents dare not upset him, or enter his room without permission. They describe this behavior as *cute* when they attempt to explain their liberal limits to their colleagues. He, like so many other teens, literally *runs* his house and knows what to do and say to manipulate his own selfish way. His parents fall for his mind games every time."

"Get to the girl Deception, for your sake this investment of time in the boy had better lead to something amusingly tragic with the girl," Satan maintained.

"Listen carefully; I'm sure you won't be disappointed. Our boy is already physically attracted to both Sandy and her best friend. He fantasizes about sex with them both. He got the idea from a recent music video he saw in which his favorite performer boasted of his own sexual escapades. And to demonstrate our "generosity" we will satisfy his longings. First with Sandy, then after he pledges to her his *unfailing love,* we will give him her best friend. From this time forward his fantasies will govern his behavior."

"Oooh Deception, sometimes you are wonderfully wicked and deliciously despicable," doted Satan.

"This scenario can be repeated multiple times in multiple ways with thousands of teens. But there is more in store for our young lovers." Deception said with a coy smile easing onto his face.

"Do tell Deception, don't keep me waiting!" said Satan, who sat up and gleamed with anticipation."

"Destroying the young lives of teenagers is of some pleasant consequence to us. This causes much grief to our Enemy as you know. But the standards of badness we settle into these lives today, allow us to reap in fruitlessness from the lives of their bloodline to the second, third and even fourth generation! We exploit the natural pattern the Enemy reveals daily in nature. Seeds reproduce after their own kind."

"Magnificent! I love it!" Satan said with exuberance. "Allow me to surmise the principle at work here Deception. Our goal is not only the life of the victim, but the *lives* within our young victim yet to even be born." Satan began to nod his head with approval. "Finally I think you've got it, Deception. I do believe you finally understand the magnitude of our potential desecration of our Enemy's most adored creation."

"Well, thank you master," Deception said with a snobby false humility. "I only learned from the best," he admitted. Satan gloated.

"Flattery will get you everywhere Deception," Satan said mischievously. "Continue please with your progress with

Sandy. How are you faring with her?"

"Sandy's mind, our battlefield, is an open door. The ease of establishing doctrines of the dark side meets all expectations. Her resistance weakens with each of her failures. Her every compromise brings her closer to our unlimited control. Nothing, serious anyway, can at this point slow our progress. Sandy, like most teens, holds absolutely no convictions about her choice of music, movies, television shows or thought life. She sees it all, listens to it all, watches it all, and most importantly, thinks of it all. She even thinks thoughts she didn't plan on thinking. Our seeds, deposited in her thought-life, are sure to produce our desire, our fruit. Like a lamb led to the slaughter unaware, Sandy follows our deception without fail. We already see it in her dress, hear it in her speech and witness it in her behavior. Can you imagine how many relationships now, and even marriages later, we shall be able to destroy because of this, independent, free-spirited girl?" Deception asked rhetorically.

"Deeeelicious, Deception. Goody! Goody! Might you be sounding just a little like me these days?" arrogantly Satan asked.

"Our work with Ronnie, sir, poses quite a rather different picture. After much manipulation we successfully compromised every intimate image of godliness in his life. Ronnie grew up in what he has only known as "the church". Thanks to diligent work by our demons Compromise, Gossip and Sedition, it's been a church in name only. For over thirty-five years it's been a church that has never fully received the…so-called Anointed One… but is well-versed in Christianity. They have settled for a comfortable position, close to the cross but far from Christ." Deception explained cautiously.

Deception was cautious because he came close to actually saying the name *Jesus*. To speak the name Jesus guaranteed immediate doom. Satan never permitted any demon, duke, prince, legion, imp, captain, low or high ranking dark spirit to ever even whisper the name of Jesus. Satan so despised that name that he established that edict as an eternal law of the dark side. The name of Jesus, may never spoken in any form or fashion on the dark side. Satan alleged that Jesus' name "poisoned" allegiance on the dark side. Well, the reasoning he purported to have told his demons differed from the truth. In actuality Satan knew his assault upon Jesus at Mt. Calvary was not a victory as he let on, but a defeat, his worst yet, his worst ever. Satan knew this same Jesus sealed his fate, eternal damnation, when he rose from the grave on the third day like he promised. Unlike any event in history, Jesus overcame Satan's greatest blow, death. Satan also knew very well that he and Jesus would meet again, in the end, and at the sound of the name of Jesus, Satan's host will witness the lord of the dark side, Satan himself, bow to the Lord of all, Jesus, and confess Him King of Kings and Lord of Lords. In a recurring frequent vision since the resurrection, Satan saw himself being led captive, bound and gagged with his accomplices Sin, Death, and the Grave all shackled together. A cheering crowd, too numerous to number, looked on and shouted praises to the Almighty God. The defeated foe, Satan, and his disarmed collaborators marched to the lake of fire. Deep within, Satan knew this dream served as certain prophecy of his inescapable destiny.

Deception continued, "Ronnie's church sir, they accentuate acts, repetitive prayers and only the shell of the truth. They prioritize the traditions of men over the truth of the Enemy, making our Enemy's word of none effect. The son of a church elder, Ronnie has seen and heard more than the average churched youth."

"Let's talk about the plan for him shall we?" asked Satan. "If we fail to plan we plan to fail! There must be a plan."

"We have arranged for his father, whom we shall refer to as our dear beloved elder, and his father's mistress to be "found out" by Ronnie's mother. To avoid the open rebuke and the embarrassment of the church, the mother, the father and the mistress made an agreement. They plan to keep the romance a secret for the sake of the family. And also for the sake of our dear beloved elders small stipend he receives from the church. That way Ronnie, his brother and sister, and mother and father could all be 'one big happy family', on the outside that is, until the children graduate from high school. What begins next is that familiar cycle so often dogging marriages, the split-up, then divorce and finally resignation and relocation."

"Excellent work Deception. I know from experience, and am confident that the emotional scarring of children deepens daily after the divorce and lasts a lifetime. Parents modeling hypocrisy on my behalf is an added delight for the dark side. It sounds great! What about the boy? What is your plan for the boy, Deception?" asked Satan.

"Thanks for asking, I'm getting to the boy. The father's mistress, a single mother, has a son at the same school as Ronnie. If all goes according to the Task Force's plan, the mistress' son unfortunately discovers his wonderful mother in a delightfully disgusting, lewd sexual encounter with our dear dysfunctional elder. Our friend Murder, encouraged by his nephew Sir Rage will see to it that the boy does not permit the Elder to leave that house alive. Violence planted the gun, Rebellion already established the course of action, and a recent *hell-o-vision* show detailed for the son not only step-by-step what to do, but how to do it and get away with it, so he thinks. It's amazing how our, *"you can get away with it"*, lie has been the downfall of so many throughout the entire history of mankind. What a perfect lie!"

"What has this to do with Ronnie?" Satan impatiently inquired.

"Get this," snickered Deception. "Our Enemy becomes his enemy. Rebellion then accesses Ronnie's battlefield, his mind, with legions of demons. A host of 2,000 are prepared to occupy as we speak. Ronnie's self-destruct sequence begins with his rebellion against his mother for her compromise, then the church for its ineffectiveness. And finally, he will then be embittered toward his father, though by then murdered and only a memory, for living a lie. His final disposition I find most rewarding, he will blame God for permitting such a tragedy to happen. The blame God game *always* works in hard-to-understand cases like these. We engineer the tragedy, God gets the blame, this is too easy. At this point this young man will spend so much of his life persecuting the church, he wouldn't recognize his gift if it hit him in the face," Deception chuckled. He then hastily covered his demonic mouth as if something had slipped out.

"What did you say spirit?" Satan Demanded.

"He's going to be on our side, he'll help us persecute the church."

"No, no, no! Not that, what did you say about a gift of some sort?" Satan asked. "Has our Enemy prepared a gift for him? Answer me you cowering nothing of a demon!" said Satan angrily.

"Sir you know that if *The Book* is correct, section four, paragraph seven of the letter to the people of Ephesus says that *everyone* has a gift. So yes sir, he has a gift like everyone else," Deception said in a low voice hoping to move on quickly here.

"But why do you fear his gift, is it special, and if so, how do you know?" asked Satan.

"I guess you could say it's special. I inadvertently discovered it at his infant dedication, sir. A man of God, a missionary attended, sent by the Holy Spirit."

"Keep talking," Satan gripped Deception tightly by the throat and pulled him nose to nose, "Speak!"

"The man of God did one of those prophecy things again," Deception croaked.

"Prophecy? I hate prophecy! Well, speak the prophecy, word for word," Satan insisted.

"But sir...word for word?" Deception asked in disbelief. "Are you sure...word for word? He asked slowly.

"WORD FOR WORD DEMON!" Satan shouted.

"As you wish sir, the man prophesied as follows," Deception deepened his voice imitating the missionary as best as he could recall. 'Thus would say the Lord God Almighty unto you. I have bestowed many gifts, saith the Lord, upon this child. And yea, he shall receive this day the greatest of his gifts, the gift of evangelism. And thus would say the Lord unto you, many, yea, even multitudes of the young shall know my name and receive my Son because of this one, saith the Lord thy God. I have given him a special anointing saith the Lord, yea, a double anointing, saith the Lord thy God. The young shall repent because of my call upon this life. And yea, as I have decreed it, I shall bring it to pass. For I am the Lord thy God and besides Me there is no other'..."

"ENOUGGGGHHH!" howled Satan interrupting. "You mean to tell me as Paul, that traitor, was assigned to the gentiles, this Ronnie has been assigned to the young? Take note!" He began to speak frantically. "We must move quickly. This really isn't fair. If only I were all-knowing these little developments would not catch me so unprepared so often. Listen closely to my anti-prophecy strategy. When we return to the lair, remind me to assign Confusion to keep this youth preoccupied with that which he doesn't understand, so much so, that complete confusion will occupy his mind. Have Corruption speak to the authorities that honor me. Among them I'm certain you'll find one willing to manipulate the system to silence this threat. I need official documentation to qualify him as emotionally unstable. Additionally, see to it that his prognosis requires him to enter the state mental institution the rest of his days. That way after his persecution of the church, his voice, will no longer be heard, by anyone, let alone the youth. Let's see if *this* prophecy survives our hindrances!"

"As you wish, it shall be done, your cruddiness, it shall be done," Deception vowed.

CHAPTER 10

Leah strained to endure the pain of the inked needle etching a unicorn tattoo, the symbol of fantasy, into her upper right arm. The only tattoo she had ever had stuck on but then washed off. This was surely not going to wash off. It was permanent, like the pledge of every other 14-year-old newcomer to the largest gang on the Southside. In the Midwest, back where she was born and raised, gangs were thought to be something bad. That's not how she found it at all. Here in the city, the gang was identity, the gang was cool, the gang was family, and the gang was acceptance and attention. For certain situations, the gang was protection and the gang was powerful. Of course there was a minor feat of initiation to be performed. She had been sworn to secrecy never to reveal her rite of initiation. That part wasn't difficult for her. She didn't want anyone to know, anyway, of the crime she had to commit to gain access to the gang. Her mom, as a single parent raised her to be a respectable young lady. Unlike the others, she was more ashamed of initiation than proud. Nevertheless she was in!

Satan turned with a puzzled look on his face. "So what's the big deal Deception? It's not like I haven't committed a young one to a gang before. I have some younger than 14 lost in the gang life."

"It's not just the fact that she's in a gang. It's the principle of our scheme that I think will appeal to you most. As you know, certain things have been set in motion that we cannot... let's say... we have difficulty stopping," said Deception carefully.

"Such as...?" asked Satan in a threatening tone.

"Such as, the truth," responded Deception. "I mean the *so-called* 'truth' he corrected himself. According to *The Book*, Jeremiah section 29, paragraph 11, the enemy states, 'I know the plans I have for you...to give you a future with hope.' Another ancient prophecy," Satan growled at that word and shook his head, "predicted that a young virgin would give birth. Thus when the young one, Mary was selected by our Enemy to be the mother of the Nazarene, she was found among virgins. She was a virgin, so they say. Our scheme is to so manipulate the lives of the young, in this case Leah, that when the prophetic reward from the Kingdom of Light appears, pointing to a future with hope, the recipient is not around, better yet no where to be found. Thus, if Leah is deep into the gang life, she won't be found where she is supposed to be when her blessing comes, unlike Mary. The Enemy does so much according to seasons and timing. We just help her miss her season or her time of blessing. Do you follow sir?"

"Pure thievery, I like it. But you can do that with any form of rebellion. Why choose a gang?"

"This is not just any gang," answered Deception. "The gang leader is one whom you've commissioned personally years ago at a black mass. He drank of the blood sacrifice and is completely evil. This young man is into it all, ouiji boards, levitation, séances, astrology, horoscope, tarot cards, the whole thing. We've arranged for Leah to fall into lust with our gang leader. Meanwhile she'll miss out on true Love when it comes calling, back where she is supposed to be. So you see, much of our destroying is not destroying at all. We simply prepare young people to miss the Enemy's blessing. For try if He will, He *cannot* bless iniquity, so iniquity it is."

CHAPTER 11

Satan and Deception returned to the lair. All the forces of the dark side frantically worked their schemes. Confusion, as ordered, prepared his troops to assault Ronnie. The special assignments to Procrastination and Forgetfulness regarding the knowledge of the promises of *The Book* were carried out in detail. Soon many young "Christian" students were ashamed of their bibles and their beliefs. Instead of changing their behavior to honor their beliefs, they modified their beliefs to accommodate their ungodly behavior. They regularly put off the reading and studying of the Word. Forgetfulness wiped the thought of reading from their minds. Church attendance was just a matter of going through the motions. Teens even refused to carry their bibles to the one place they were sure to need it, church. The Teenage Task Force was in full force. Rebellion conditioned through media. Lust manipulated hormones. The Children's Defense Fund discovered that one out of every sixteen teenage girls became mothers before leaving high school. In some communities that ratio reached as high as one in every nine. Premature teenage fathers ignored the responsibility of raising their children. Just like the videos, male enough to make a baby but not man enough to raise a child. Satan was repeatedly successful in removing the male from the home. Children were abandoned by their fathers to be raised by their mothers, just as the Task Force anticipated. Drug use among teens rose like never before. Of the 3,000 teens that began smoking each day, 1,000 would eventually die. Eight thousand teenagers a day lost their virginity. Three thousand each day became pregnant. One thousand babies a day were aborted from their teenage mothers. The Centers for Disease Control reported that 200 teenagers contracted sexually transmitted diseases every thirteen minutes. In certain areas, sexually transmitted diseases increased 500% over the next few years. The incidence of HIV infection among the young rose steadily over each month. Seventy-five percent of the youth in gangs had criminal records. Violence stepped up his work. In one year 129,000 juveniles were arrested for violent crimes as recorded by the United States Justice Department. It was the highest in history with 3,300 arrested for murder. In one year alone, 6,300 youths were arrested for forcible rape, 45,700 for robbery and 74,000 for aggravated assault. Teens as victims of homicide doubled from four per 100,000 to eight per 100,000, for an average of seven teens murdered per day. Each murdered teen represented four generations of a family that would never exist. The rate of teen suicide increased 31%. Every 2 hours and 16 minutes one teenager committed suicide. Satan called the Teenage Task Force to a victory celebration. The room was filled with howling demons hissing and growling at one another.

"I propose a toast," said the devil, standing with a wide-mouth grin plastered across his face, "To the deceit of Deception and his mighty band of demons at their finest hour." Just then a frantic, frail demon rushed to Deception's side.

"Sir, we must talk," he said.

"Not now," Deception said. "Can't it wait?"

"I'm afraid not sir, we must speak," the demon hissed. Deception smacked the demon then lifted his chalice to join the toast. "IT'S ABOUT JAMES!" shouted the demon loud enough for everyone to hear. The room fell quiet. The music scratched to a screeching stop. The applause and laughter died out.

"What do you have to report imp," Satan disrespectfully demanded before Deception could respond.

"It's James sir, from the test case. They've added a new course to the curriculum this year at his school, drafting," the demon replied.

"You interrupted my party to bother me with an insignificant drafting class", Satan laughed with disbelief." The others joined Satan in a courtesy chuckle.

"Wait sir," pleaded Deception. "Remember, James has architectural tendencies and drafting is a core course for architects."

"So get him kicked out of class or expelled from school," Satan demanded.

"But that's not all of it sir," the demon said shyly. "The teacher is a believer."

"Is he just a believer, or a Belieeeeever-Believer?" Satan asked, now rendering his full attention to the demon.

"I would say he's a Belieeeeever-Believer. We can't touch him or come near his class. It's filled with Holy fire," said the demon, "the fire that does not consume." The satanic hosts gasped in amazement.

"Hmm, a true Agent, and James, how is he responding?" asked Deception with concern.

"It's his *favorite* class and *favorite* teacher. The teacher loves his students like a father." Before the demon could finish his sentence, immediately Procrastination rushed in.

"We can't get *The Book* away from James," he panted desperately trying to catch his breath. "His teacher gave him a new one with study helps and teenage stuff in it this morning. He loves it."

"*The Book!*" yelled Satan, "he gave James *The Book*? However did he get one of those things in that building without our harassment?" he fretted.

"We don't know sir, Procrastination replied, he must have snuck it in after hours. One of those disgusting ambitious Fellowship of Christian Athletes kids has been passing them out at meetings; perhaps he got *The Book* from them. Those students are quite knowledgeable on student-led, student-run equal access laws."

"Drats!" Satan cursed, his eyes rummaged around the atmosphere seeking an appropriate response. "Go back! Take Anger, Jealousy and Perversion with you. ATTACK, ATTACK!" Satan said frantically. "To whoever can somehow reverse these recent turn of events I will grant to sit at my right hand." There was a commotion at the back of the room followed by ghastly loud shrieks.

"HELP....HELP!" cried two badly beaten demons, rushing in to report. "We tried to stop it but they were too many".

"WHO WERE TOO MANY?" cried Satan, beginning to look worried. "SPEAK UP YOU FOOLS!" Satan shouted with a sense of fear and helplessness in his eyes.

"THE GUARDIANS!," said the first demon barely breathing.

"Tell me what happened and to whom," demanded Satan.

"The boy…the boy escaped. He escaped…to the path of righteousness. The boy is now an Agent…" said the second demon just before collapsing to the floor. Several demons fluttered to his side, not to assist him but only to scavenge for his powers.

"What boy?" asked Satan slowly with rage in his voice turning to Deception.

"The mistress' son, he who was supposed to murder Ronnie's father, our dysfunctional elder," cried the first demon.

"What do you mean *supposed* to?" asked Satan.

"It was scheduled to happen tomorrow," interrupted Deception. KICK! Satan kicked the little messenger demon against the wall with the heel of his hoofed foot in a fierce rage.

"You had better have a good explanation or I'll have you pummeled to a bloody pulp. HOW DID THE BOY ESCAPE?" Satan roared.

"We assembled in a safe place," he began slowly and breathing deeply, "the school auditorium. We patiently awaited the beginning of an average school assembly with a football hero to speak. When he arrived at least forty mighty guardian angels escorted him into position. We suspected then he was an Agent. There was no time to solicit back-up. Besides, as I said, the auditorium was safe. The fire that does not consume blazed everywhere he stepped, keeping us away from the stage. We didn't understand at first," the demon gasped trying to find the oxygen to finish his explanation. "We thought that nothing could violate our church and state clause. There were only eight of us, and as you can see only two returned. He began to speak about his life as a football hero and all the benefits of money and materialism. We made sure that the attractiveness of the superficial sunk deep into the young hearts. He alluded to the importance of role models. We rejoiced thinking he was modeling materialism himself. But as their hearts opened wide with laughter and intrigue, he tricked us. He did the unexpected," the demon said with wide eyes and disbelief. "He asked for questions right in the middle of his talk. No one ever does that! A respected senior class young woman on the volleyball team asked him to identify his mentor and role model. The next moment he spoke the name of the Lamb of God, The forbidden name. We couldn't believe it! Impossible!" the demon agonized. "He told the students, 'My role model has also been my best friend. He taught me how to be a husband, father, and a man of character and integrity', yada, yada, yada, more stuff like that. He then said, 'My role model is my big brother...', and he then said the forbidden name of the Nazarene! As we feared, the footballer was an Agent. We immediately tried to distract our target, the mistress's son, but it was too late. The Spirit of the Enemy had full control. We dashed toward the principal to suggest the 'church and state' violation, or maybe remind him of the pressure the Parent Teachers Association was sure to bear upon him, but in an instant the guardians surrounded us. They were big, powerful and full of light. Fighting them was futile. I have never met guardians like these before, sir, never," cried the demon with false tears hoping to provoke sympathy from the dark master. "Their glance alone incinerated two of our monitors who passed fatally too close to the footballer, hear me, THEIR GLANCE ALONE! Four others suffocated in the heat of the non-consuming fire. The sight of our colleagues in a heap of ashes near the stage paralyzed us with fear; our very own survival depended upon our hasty exit."

"What about Ronnie, the elder's son? I assume Ronnie was there, this was a full-school mandatory assembly, was it not", inquired Satan.

"Yes sir," said the demon.

"Report, you fool, before I destroy you for bringing me such bad news," Satan said.

"As we speak Ronnie is preparing to hear the football hero himself again at a local church tonight."

"LEGIONS, LEGIONS!" Satan quickly summoned a host of demons to come forward representing at least twenty-five thousand. "You and your wicked horde must attend that meeting. DO-NOT-LET-THAT-BOY-BOW-HIS-KNEES!!! WE MUST HINDER! Stop the Agent, stop his car, attack his throat, attack the service, distract! DISTRACT! DISTRACT!" Satan shouted.

"But sir, the guardians, won't they surely show up there? I'm sure they won't be as gracious this time around," the battered demon spoke in terror.

"EITHER YOU DEAL WITH THESE GUARDIANS OR YOU DEAL WITH MEEEEEE!!!" Satan spoke coldly with the fire and fierceness of a dragon. Immediately a host of demons took flight. Another demon came to report.

"Sir.... sir it's Sandy's boyfriend, he's acting weird," said the demon.

"What do you mean weird?" asked Satan apprehensively. "Come on, out with it".

"Whenever he visits Sandy, the dark one inside of him begins to squirm. He can't even sit still."

"Why doesn't he just leave like all the other victims when in church, or other instances where that despicable light shines on my glorious darkness," prodded Satan.

"He does leave. Normally, we'll give him a lie or some other excuse to exit. But for some reason he keeps returning. There's something in that house that attracts him other than Sandy," the demon responded. "He keeps singing a silly song about life without Jeezzz...I mean the "Nazarene" is like a donut, there's a whole in the middle your heart. I don't understand him at all or this donut thing." Satan grew weary. He of course recognized the childhood sing-song that played in the mind of Sandy's friend. He despised the seed so often planted by God that surmised that life without Jesus is like a donut, because there's a whole in the middle of your heart. No matter how many the years, children rarely forgot the melody or the words.

Satan, in an attempt to keep his assaults from unraveling, asked, "Is our plan still intact?"

"We've encountered a problem there too, sir," the demon reluctantly continued. "The seduction was supposed to begin last night but because of his respect for Sandy's mother, he couldn't bring himself to spoil Sandy's virginity.

Instead, he's going over to Sandy's house tonight to discuss with her mother why she's so different and what attracts him so, about coming to that house."

Though he did not know it, his soul was homesick for an intimate knowledge of its Creator. The perversion in his life disagreed with his conscience. Clearly a part of him longed to hold Sandy, kiss her, and even fulfill with her, his deep fantasies of sex and the profane he's rehearsed countless times in his mind. Instead, the most perplexing contradictions of emotions raged on. Yearning to do whatever to get whatever from her battled his reverent respect of her and his thirst to hear more from her mom. Something about that house spoke to a part of him that he did not know even existed. His soul yearned for new life.

"*Holy Ground*," mumbled Satan.

"What did you say sir?" asked the demon.

"*HOLY GROUND*" Satan shouted. "Sandy's mother is a prayer warrior and has obviously declared her home, *Holy Ground*! She undoubtedly has gathered with other Agents to intensify that non-consuming fire in her house. You must keep the boy away from the house. Change all plans. Do not let him near the house. All that we must do between him and Sandy must be provided for elsewhere. WORK, DEMON! MOVE! WE MUST NOT, NAY, WE CANNOT GIVE UP. Some things I may not see until it's too late, but this one thing I do know, there is only one place I prefer never to do battle if at all possible….*Holy Ground*.

CHAPTER 12

Deception raised a talon to speak. Satan turned his head in disgust and said, "If it's not good news I don't want to hear it."

"Sir," Deception began with a hint of confidence." I've gotten notice that Leah has entered our trap as planned. Her closest friends tricked her into going to a party to meet our gang leader. You know the one; he drank of the sacrifice and bows to worship you."

"Oh yes," said Satan, "the little evil one. Is he open and prepared to commit assault and rape?"

"Yes sir, he is. This is neither his first conquest nor his last," said Deception.

That afternoon Leah joined her friends at a "party". Deception provided Leah with a popular teenage pattern; telling your parents you're one place but actually going to another. She told her mother she would be "baby-sitting". Her friends persisted and persuaded her to attend the party. She thought it funny though, when she arrived, that she found no one there but her friends, or so it seemed. Her best friend pointed to the back room telling her, "Someone wants to talk to you." Trusting her friends completely, knowing that they "had her back", Leah cautiously headed for the room in the back. She opened the door and stepped inside. The dark, musty room made Leah sick to her stomach. The gang leader used that spot for one thing and one thing only. Leah found herself on the verge of discovering the rooms' purpose. Once inside, the door closed gently. The gang leader, at first behind the door, now stood silently behind Leah with his back to the door. In the dim lighting she immediately recognized his face but not the sinister expression he wore.

"You down with the crew?" he asked.

"I'm down," she replied, still a little concerned about the emptiness in his eyes.

"True to death?" he asked.

"True to death!" she answered as she had learned in her initiation.

"Take off your clothes sweetheart," he demanded.

"What do you...what do you mean, take off my clothes? I don't think I can do that...I'm not ready for that!" She pleaded.

"That tattoo on your arm says that you *are* ready and you will do anything for the crew." She headed for the door. He quickly locked it and pocketed the key. He snatched her into his arms. He easily overpowered her young innocent body. She fought, pounded and kicked on the door. She tried to scream but he covered her lips quickly with his big, dirty, crusty palm only before forcing his mouth over hers. She smelled the alcohol on his breath. He pressed his body against hers. She smelled the stale stench of marijuana on his clothes. She hated it. She hated everything. She tried to stay strong but soon began to cry and continued to fight desperately. Her weary arms failed her now – her knees bowed from the twisted tension as she pressed her torso back and forward to escape his grip. Tired from struggling, growing weak from the strain to resist, she gave in. Her body simply caved-in under the physical force of his constant badgering. In the other room she heard her best friends snickering and giggling as the gang leader had his way with "their girl", Leah. Leah forced herself to only think of the comfort and love of her home. She felt as if that home was a thousand miles away. Her mind began to drift as she attempted to blackout the numbness of her deflowering. So embarrassingly deceived by her close friends, Leah realized the only truth of which she was certain…. "mother would never let this happen to her baby". And although she and her mom had their differences, she realized much too late that her only true friend in the entire world was…mom. Her "friends", the very ones, who pledged their unending allegiance, ignored her in her time of desperate need. Her friends knew that the gang leader intended to violently rape her. They endured the same degrading experience. They knew Leah would, like them, pay the same high price of her honor and self respect to appease the gang leader. They were not aware however of the full extent of this wicked young man's plan. After he had finished with Leah he headed for the closet door. Three other members of the crew were watching and waiting for their turn. The gang leader hesitated. He looked at Leah. She stared back blankly with sad helpless eyes. Seeing her there used, abused, bleeding and whimpering, a spark of compassion flickered in his heart. But after a long, pondering gaze, he then thought of his childhood and how his mother hated him every second of his life for resembling his father. The hatred he had for his mother seemed to engulf him again. In fact, as he looked upon Leah, his mind started playing tricks on him. Leah's face began to morph into the image of his mother, like a mirage, just as other women's faces had done whom he violated before in his life. He hated his mother with a pure hatred, mostly because she hated him so intensely. Slowly at first, then growing in volume a monstrous demon, the spirit of Hatred himself, began whispering, then shouting.

"Do her..., Do Her..., DO HER! DO HER!" The force of the voice of Hatred quickly extinguished the gang leader's weak spark of compassion as his countenance turned wickedly hateful. He turned to "his boys" who came from the closet and said in a fierce forceful tone, "DO HER!" The boys exited the closet. Standing over Leah something very peculiar happened. It seem as though Leah was seductively beckoning the boys to continue. The gang symbol of the unicorn tattooed on Leah housed the spirit of fantasy. Fantasy tricked the boys by camouflaging Leah's helpless body with a fantasy vision of what they wanted to see. The young boys quickly took their turns, with Leah's listless, nearly lifeless, dead to her danger, body.

Satan slapped hands with Deception as they laughed at Leah.

"I like how her girlfriend said, 'I didn't hear you banging on no door. I must have had the TV turned up too loud'," Satan mimicked. "I also like how you housed the spirit of fantasy within the unicorn tattoo. I had almost forgotten the grounds that tattoos give their spirits to live. That, my dear boy, was a good touch. My Deception today wasn't a total loss after all. I was beginning to feel a little like Job. Remember what we did to him?" Deception laughed before nodding in response.

CHAPTER 13

Despite his short-lived celebration with Deception, the dramatic sequence of the day's events troubled Satan. Deep inside Satan tried to ignore the sickening feeling in his stomach eerily similar to the one he experienced some 2000 years ago, the day the word from the grave declared that Jesus arose and lived. Neither his most artistic nor creative lies could produce the body of the one whose tomb the world found empty. After suffering his gruesome death on the cross and being raised on the third day, the Son of God returned to His Father and His throne snatching the keys to death and hell from Satan along the way. Something about this Task Force, the strategy, and the case studies just did not settle well with Satan. A barrage of words, comments spoken by the Lamb, plagued his mind. "Woman, where are thy accusers?" "Someone touched me!" "She is not dead only sleeping!" "Be thou made whole!" "All power has been given unto me..." "Receive thy sight!" "Why persecuteth thou me?"

"Hoowwwl," Satan let out a deep howl! It riveted the residents of the dark side. Breathing heavily and sensing doom, he looked to Deception, and shrieked in a panic, "Jaaames! JAAAAMES! Where is JAMES?" he summoned Deception, with eyes a fierce blood red, nostrils flared, and sulfuric smoke steaming from his mouth. He sensed that he had better check up on his teenage victims. The Holy One was at work. He felt it. He knew it and his intuition proved absolutely correct. James' teacher initiated deep conversations about eternity, purpose and destiny. He also spoke into James' life, by labeling him talented and gifted and by assuring him of his bright future. In fact, the Holy Spirit had revealed to the teacher concerning James that God prepared a specific plan for James' life. He then told James that he identified a strong leadership gifting on his life, not a follower, the head, not the tail. James started believing in himself, taking a stand, setting the standard and studying...*The Book.*

"I don't know what happened sir. I can't explain it!" squeaked Deception.

"Deception, you need not explain, let me guess, we're failing," Satan said deflated.

"Something like that sir."

"And Ronnie?" asked Satan without energy.

"As you know sir, we lost the mistresses' son to the path of righteousness. He went on to be baptized that evening at the local church. The football hero performed the service," confessed Deception.

"You're boring me with details. What's the real damage?" Satan blurted impatiently.

"We can't seem to stop the mistresses' son from talking about his 'new life'. He's telling *everybody*, his friends, his enemies and even his teachers. And just as we feared, boldness and zeal characterize his speech and attitude. He allows no tradition to go unquestioned nor the status quo unchallenged. He destroys his comfort zone with radical, almost scandalous ambition, truly unashamed. Almost a supernatural courage empowers him to 'rock the boat'. It's all so sickening," Deception said in defeat with disgust.

"What about Ronnie, Deception? Get to the point. Do we have him or don't we?" Satan insisted.

"Sir," Deception continued, "the mistress has repented because of her son's testimony."

Led by the Spirit, the mistress, broken in spirit, visited for the first time the home of her one time secret love, the beloved elder. "This is insane", she thought to herself but if her son could be bold about his new faith so could she. Unsure of what to say and why to even approach the wife of the man with whom she entered adultery, something within compelled her to continue. When Ronnie's' mother answered the door, an awkward silence loud as a sonic boom froze the moment. The mistress humbled herself, and with deep, sincere emotion apologized and appealed for forgiveness. Amidst tremendous tension, the two women searched for an understanding and a reason to remain in dialogue. The two women cried, prayed, vented and repented. Anger turned to pity, wrath was squelched by peace. Thanks to the touch of the Great Healer, scars were turned to stars. Ronnie's' mother in an unexpected gesture asked for forgiveness for all of the ill feelings she felt toward the mistress, knowing of her husband's indiscretions. She then confessed that she more than likely lost her husband long ago and was resolved today to do what was right rather than what seemed reasonable. The two then talked with tear stain faces all night long stopping intermittently for prayer. Although they had shared the same man, ironically they found themselves more like sisters than enemies. For the first time Ronnie witnessed the Enemy's unconditional love in his family, and the Love that passes all understanding in his home.

Deception reported on Ronnie, "He keeps repeating something he heard from the football hero. It's not something that we like to hear…'Greater is He that is in you than he that is in the world'."

"Stop it!" Satan blurted, embarrassed by his voice cracking like a pubescent middle school-er. "I know the rest", he said after clearing his throat.

"Though he yet resists bowing his knees to our Enemy, he toys repeatedly with the idea of surrender." Deception cautioned.

"Back to the Teenage Task Force, we need to re-focus our evil. There is still hope for Ronnie. Keep him thinking and pondering. That will delay hearing and obeying. As long as he is thinking and pondering, he won't hear nor act on the Enemy's voice or obey His commands. There's hope for Ronnie," Satan said.

"But not for Sandy's boyfriend," interjected Deception. "We failed in our efforts to keep him from the house."

"WHAT!" screamed Satan in phony surprise?

"I have just received an urgent communication from the battlefront. As you said sir, Sandy's mother declared her home *Holy Ground*. The fire that does not consume surrounded the entire house last night. We couldn't even come close. We could barely recognize what transpired inside. Sandy's mother led him to the path of righteousness. The boy is now an Agent!

Sandy's mother explained that good always overcomes evil, the liar! She even equipped the boy with a personalized copy of *The Book*. We did everything possible to prevent it." Deception bowed his head in response to the setback, like a pitcher giving up a grand slam homerun.

"What type classification of *The Book* did she give?"

"As we feared, it was the appropriate student version, in the class of Fellowship of Christian Athletes handy camp bible. And this boy, I'm afraid is devouring this text. He even sleeps with it."

"Assign the follow-up team to immediately challenge the boy's escape. The last thing we need is another fiery teenage Agent on our hands. We'll see how long he lasts under attack from the faithfulness of my dear friend Doubt," Satan schemed. "Complicate the experience. Dishearten him with thoughts of the difficulty of a successful walk on the path of righteousness."

"But sir, you and I both know that as long as he believes, his faith, even as small as a mustard seed, guarantees success on the path of righteousness..."

"SHUT - UP!!" Satan cut - in. "JUST DO AS YOU ARE COMMANDED DEMON!" After a long pause and a long look of deep consternation Satan continued speaking. "I hate to make this request because I know he's our most over-worked demon. Our valuable commodity of time dwindles with each wasted second. I'm afraid once again we must summon the Duke of Discouragement to preserve our chances at this stage. Bring our handsome comrade the Duke of Discouragement at once! When overwhelmed by Discouragement, the boy will return. We may be able to make another pass at seducing Sandy later."

"There was uncovered at least one consolation; we were able to convince Sandy that her mom *stole* her boyfriend. That way the bridge between she and her mom will remain strained and at best severed." Deception said with hope.

"And how did you manage that?" asked Satan.

"Easy." Deception continued." We showed it to her on one of our afternoon talk shows, The Nikki Black Show. We explained to her that the exact same drama she witnessed on her *hell-o-vision* indeed happened to her. She believed that ridiculous lie enough to even cuss her mother with venomous words of hate and accusations. Teenagers, like Sandy, who reject the truth we find most vulnerable to accept our most profound lies. We successfully laid some significant groundwork for Sandy. But the boy," deception said shaking his head with an emphatic no, "unless the follow-up team sees success, I fear our attempts and attacks on him simply wastes our time. Perhaps the most expeditious use of our energy and resources calls for our giving up on this kid and pursuing another candidate."

"Give up? NEVER! Satan shouted. I give up on no one! If it takes years, I don't give up, ever!"

"But sir, All of our footholds and strongholds departed the boy. He's full of the Holy fire."

"No way, full of the fire already? But he's just converted. What about Lust and Perversion? I thought their strongholds crushed his free will!" Satan inquired.

"Yes sir, our wickedness made significant in-roads, but

at his conversion our Enemy awarded this boy all of the benefits of The Kingdom of God immediately, unfortunately that also included deliverance. That prayer warrior wielded specific promises and privileges of *The Book*. She moved swiftly without hesitation like a very skilled warrior. She exposed every darkness in his life and expelled every representative demon. In fact, her explanation of 'grace' ultimately rescued the lad from our grasp." Deception trembled in fear as he saw Satan rise.

CRUNCH! Satan's hand sunk deep into the face of Deception. Satan's violent response demonstrated his true self. The sum of evils, a thief, a dragon, a serpent, a vile, ruthless, foul devil, Satan proved disloyal even to his own demons. Satan, destined **NEVER** to know the benefits of God's *eternal grace* fumed angrily. He knew too well of the Almighty's relentless love and sufficient grace, made available for everyone. God's grace remained obtainable to all. It did not matter who you were or what your background. It did not matter who you did or did not know, or how much money, friends or influence you did or did not enjoyed. It did not matter how shallow or deep ones excursion into sin extended. There is nothing you can do to make God love you more. By the same token, there is nothing you can do that can make God love you less. His love for His creation is perfect and His grace sufficient. Satan exists as the only entity outside of God's stretch of grace. As Lucifer, he once worshipped on God's Holy Mountain. He witnessed God's pure compassion, and His forgiving heart. He beheld mercy hand in hand with grace surrounding God's throne. Satan understands, yet can do nothing about the fact that God holds no grudges. His free grace is always offered and always deep enough to cover the deepest sin. Satan also knew that he forfeited God's grace eternally on the day he aspired to be higher than God, the day he aimed to have the God of the universe bow to him. It would never happen. For that day God cast Satan down from heaven, like a lightening bolt. That day, Lucifer, now Satan, along with one third of the angels began their miserable existence, eternally separated from the Holy God.

CHAPTER 14

It was a murky, slimy, dismal grim day in the habitat of the dark side. Satan's host found themselves battered, torn and beaten, repelled and defanged by the Prince of Peace and the mighty host of the Lord. Satan's greatest fear was now sweeping through the land like wildfire, **Revival**! Initiated by the young, teenagers reclaimed their schools, communities and homes. They were warring a holy war like never before. They exercised peer-evangelism tactical advances leading their friends to the path of righteousness. A flood of new teenage Agents joined the ranks of the righteous in dismissing the Teenage Task Force. Students became selective in their television viewing habits. They burned the tapes and CD's that poisoned and conditioned their battlefield against the heart of God. Instead, they listened to relevant attractive music of their time with strong honorable lyrics. They put down alcohol, drugs, and guns and picked up their bibles. They stopped perpetrating and began praying. They started dropping their false images and began embracing their true selves. They changed their worldly norms to godly lifestyles. Students started promoting and celebrating *saved* sex – complete abstinence, instead of *safe* sex, realizing that there really isn't any safe sex outside of marriage. Students stood up for righteousness. Students, completely unashamed of the gospel, no longer tolerated irrelevant and ineffective frozen churches and vain worship experiences. As the spark and the fire that ushered new life, the youth brought a freshness to worship. Like new wine seeking new wine skins, fresh fire was poured out over these babes in Christ, sparking revival everywhere. Dreams, visions and prophecies flowed from them like never before, like rivers of living water.

Revival became revolution due largely to the establishment of Youth Revolution Boot Camps. Spiritual warfare retreat centers designed specifically and uniquely by teenage consultants for teenagers, located throughout the country. The lifeblood of this Holy Counter-culture surge emanated from these centers. James Winfred helped in their construction as the lead young adult architect intern. James, at seventeen, failing high school and just about to drop out of school, met a drafting teacher who changed his life. The teacher shared Jesus Christ with him. James trusted Jesus and started believing in himself for the first time. The teacher told James of his giftedness and purpose. James heard then for the first time of his value. He learned of his inborn purpose and destiny. In dedication to his drafting teacher, James presented and won a proposal to develop a school for potential architects who could not afford mainstream training. Most of the retreat centers employed these young architect interns for their construction designs and insights. Many exciting youth evangelists and communicators frequented the retreat centers.

Because of the innovative and attractive designs of the centers, the youth kept coming back time after time, bringing their friends. Thousands of lives were changed year-round.

Each retreat center was customized with wave pools and water parks, athletic fields and ball courts, ropes courses, top-of-the-line sound systems, video movie theaters, training and teaching rooms, prayer chapels, Biblical libraries, outreach centers, service centers, roller skating and ice skating rinks, horseback riding, parachuting, weight lifting and weight training rooms, walking track, hiking trails, and a host of scheduled and non-scheduled activities.

A spontaneous relationship developed between professional athletes and the ongoing work of the Youth Revolution Centers. Authentic believers either current or former professional athletes spoke often, conducted workshops and seminars, and shared their testimonies at the retreat centers. The coordinator of the pro-athletes component also happens to be a powerful influence in the sharing of the gospel to the young.

God regularly manifested His power through this willing vessel. Evangelist Ronnie Banks, the son of a church elder reached youth like no one else. Ronnie grew up in the church but didn't meet Christ until a personal crisis threatened the unity of his family. Ronnie attracted youth like a "pied piper". They easily identified with him and related to his way of talking and sharing. He had a double anointing of God upon his life. His unparalleled effectiveness in sharing the love of Jesus Christ simply changed lives. He quickly discerned the condition of the heart, then spoke the right words at the right times. He spoke words of wholeness to the broken, words of joy to sorrowful, and words of order to the confused. He spoke God's words.

On one occasion, an unusually mature young woman, for her age, attended the retreat center bringing several youth from the community. As a teen she experienced a brutal rape while in a short-lived gang life. She now devotes her life to helping students particularly young girls, bypass the gang life. While at the main session on Saturday night, Ronnie being led by the Spirit invited those clinging to unforgiven hurts to come down front for prayer. He explained that unforgiveness breeds bitterness. He likened unforgiveness to swallowing poison and waiting on the other person to die. His word resonated with the woman. She even thought, "It seems like there is no one here and he's talking directly to me." This woman, a community youth chaperone knew she needed to pray. The young woman moved to the front along with several of her students during Ronnie's appeal for a response.

The students called their chaperone Ms. Leah. Abused by four teenage boys at only 14 years old, Leah lost her self esteem and dignity that day. She never really knew peace of mind or forgiveness in her heart since that tragedy. She just committed her life to helping young people misled like the Leah of long ago. Somehow Ronnie knew. He discerned something different going on with this young woman, something peculiar. He stepped through the crowd at the altar. Drawn supernaturally to her he looked directly at her. He said, "I don't know you my sister, but when I look at you I see a mighty woman of God. I see royalty in you. But I sense that you don't see what I and probably others around you recognize. The Lord is saying there's a wall of shame that limits your growth. There's a beautiful person trying to smile but the darkness of your past has a spiritual choke-hold on your joy." Leah bowed her head humbly and shyly. "How does he know?" She thought to herself. Ronnie didn't know, the Lord of hosts, Jesus knew. Jesus, by his spirit, planned to free Leah. Little did she know, not only had she been raped several years ago but the act served as a spiritual doorway for demonic oppression. Not only did the rapists take her self-esteem several years ago, they also deposited the corrupt spiritual seed of their wickedness. Discouragement, the chief demon holding her joy hostage, often told her she didn't deserve to be happy or to be loved. When Ronnie stood close to Leah, she began to feel ill. Ronnie agitated the demons that had been holding her peace and joy captive for all these years. "May I pray for you, my sister?" Ronnie asked.

"Yes, I have some bitterness and unforgiveness I need to release," she said. Although her mouth said yes to the prayer, another part of her just wanted to run. The influence of the dark side simply revealed it's reluctance to be exposed attempting to compel her to run away in a panic.

"Have you asked Jesus into your heart?" Ronnie asked Leah.

"Yes I have, but sometimes I feel like I can't smile. Sometimes I don't want to smile. Sometimes I don't even want to live," she said, with shame in her voice.

Ronnie recognized the story, he'd heard it before, and the lies, he'd heard them too. "You're suffering from some spiritual oppression. You have the right to call on the name of Jesus to help you destroy the strongholds of bitterness and unforgiveness and overthrow the darkness in your life. Jesus gave his life so that the miscues of your past and the disappointments of your todays do not prevent true joy, peace and happiness from coming your way. Jesus came to set the captives free." Ronnie stepped closer to Leah, facing her, holding both of her hands to agree with her in prayer. Others from the ministry team joined together in praying for her complete victory. As they bowed their heads Ronnie paused, then nodded in agreement with a confident smile. In the spirit realm Ronnie saw something no one else did, a glorified *spirit being* standing directly behind Leah. He had his hand on Leah's shoulder with his head bowed like everyone else. God had shown Ronnie this before. Ronnie had always assumed it was a guardian angel of some sort. Ronnie had no idea, it was Jesus himself.

"Good always prevails. Greater is he that is in you than he that is in the world. Let's pray together. In the mighty name of Jesus, my big brother, I command you Satan to loose your hold on this woman of God! For the pure, holy and undefiled blood of Jesus is against you Satan. Tonight, Jesus is again our chain-breaker! Our Lord Jesus defeated you at the cross and we take authority over you and your influence in this woman's life! Greater is he that is in us than he that is in the world. This is holy ground, and you have to go. I bind the strongman now; you and all of your influence in *this* life must pack your bags and go! BE GONE, IN THE NAME OF JESUS!" Immediately, the heaviness departed Leah that had stolen her smile for years. Her heart and spirit felt light. She couldn't describe it. She felt the presence of the Holy Spirit, warm then hot, almost like a *non-consuming fire* flooding her being from the crown of her head to the soles of her feet. The hurt and bitterness departed, joy and forgiveness flushed her being. Leah, overcome with tears of joy, raised her hands in gratitude.

"Thank you Jesus for setting me free! Thank you! Thank you, Lord", Leah exclaimed as if born anew. Leah rejoiced. She melted in appreciation at the alter with a new joy in her heart and spirit. Several of the young girls from her community joined her at the alter and warmed her with hugs. She thanked Jesus for being her friend. She went on to be discipled at the center on weekends, and worked there as a volunteer at special events. She grew in wisdom and stature. She loved reading and studying the Word of God. She also memorized the promises. She helped many teenage girls who had been robbed of their virginity to acknowledge a secondary virginity and to free themselves from the grip of the dark one.

Her friendship with Ronnie grew. She adored the man of God in him, who turned out to be God's man for her. Ronnie too, adored the woman of God he saw in Leah, who as God had planned, turned out to be God's woman for him. And at the *Appointed Time* they married. Today, as Leah Banks, she and her husband evangelize the youth of the country ensuring youthful, zealous revival.

Sandy, on the other hand, blamed her mother for turning her boyfriend into a "religious freak". She left home shortly after graduation. She disappeared for years.

Again, deep in the recesses of the dark side, Satan addresses his captains. "Most of you know, of course, that the destruction of the Kingdom of Light depends entirely upon this work. I must assume, therefore, that you are prepared to report your findings. Who has the address of this young woman… Sandy?…"

The End.

EPILOGUE

Will you survive the ultimate battle? Or are you just 'going with the flow'. Any dead fish can go with the flow. It takes a live fish to go upstream. Your Creator has a rich investment in you, His Son, and a great destiny for you, life and life more abundantly. But you must be prepared to survive "The Battle". You must understand that God loves you relentlessly. He patiently waits for the return of the love and devotion He has demonstrated toward you. He proved that He loved you, for while you were yet lost in this world, and lost in sin, He sent His only Son to pay the price for your sin with His Life. What will it take for you to give up on the image of the person you are trying to be and give-in to the image of the One in whom you were made, God Almighty. There is nothing new under the sun. Satan is just as real today as he was when he nailed Jesus to the cross. He's trying just as hard to nail you to defeat. Because you are the apple of God's eye, you are loaded with potential. And when teamed with Jesus, filled with His Holy Spirit, and under the direction of the will of God, you are an Agent of God, *Armed and Dangerous,* and therefore, Satan's most feared opponent. And just as the Grave, the Cross, and Death failed to hold Jesus down, so too will Fear, Lust, Violence, Rebellion, Corruption, Abortion, Procrastination, Forgetfulness, Distraction and the chief demon himself, Satan, <u>all</u> fail to hold you back from your *Appointed time* of blessing. There is a blueprint for your life! There is a plan! It can be done! Your victory is already won, you have to walk in it. The Spirit of the King of Kings, and Lord of Lords will be with you, around you and before you. Then you will not only survive, but conquer! If that's what you want, pray this prayer with me:

Dear God, forgive me of my sins. I confess all the things that I've said or done that have displeased you. I am truly sorry. I believe you sent your son Jesus for me, born of a virgin. I believe that He died on a Cross. I believe He rose on the third day. I believe He's coming back for me. Come into my heart Jesus. Reveal your purposes for my life. Show me my destiny in you. Teach me to be strong and wise. I may not be perfect, Lord, but I can be faithful. I denounce all affiliation with the dark side. I reclaim any area of my life that Satan has stolen. My mind, heart and body all belong now to Jesus Christ. Restore my purity. I reclaim my battlefield, my mind. Fill me with the fire that does not consume. I am holy ground. I am saved by faith right now! I am born again! Jesus Himself protects me. His sinless blood, shed at the cross seals my victory. I will survive "The Battle", in Jesus name.

Amen!

Greater is He that is in you, than he that is in the world!

No Fear!